In the 1920s and 1930s
the most obvious sym
his countrymen of the
emergence as a succes
after centuries of Germaniza
As a journalist, playwi
essayist, translator, children's writer,
poet and short story writer, his literary output
was prolific and diverse. His works include plays
such as *R.U.R., From the Life of the Insects,
The Makropulos Affair* and novels such as
War with the Newts, Hordubal, Meteor
and *An Ordinary Life.*

Geoffrey Newsome played a significant role
in educational institutions in the Czech Republic
immediately after the fall of Communism.
He is author of a Czech textbook and founder
of the award-winning on-line
bookshop pickabook.co.uk.

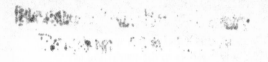

LETTERS FROM

ENGLAND
by
Karel Čapek

with illustrations by the author

translated by Geoffrey Newsome
with a foreword by Roger Scruton

A Claridge Press Book

continuum

Continuum
The Tower Building   15 East 26th Street
11 York Road   New York
London SE1 7NX   NY 10010

www.continuumbooks.com

A translation from the Czech original of Karel Čapek's *Anglické
Listy* with the author's original illustrations. The right of Geoffrey
Newsome to be identified as the translator of this work has been
asserted by him in accordance with the Copyright, Designs and
Patents Act 1998.

First published in Prague in 1924 and in Britain in 1925. Sale
forbidden by the Germans in 1939 and later by the Communists.
Reprinted in Britain in 1941 and 1951.

This edition first published in hardback by Claridge Press in 2001.
First published in paperback by Continuum 2004.

Cover illustration by Karel Čapek.
73 illustrations by Karel Čapek, and one by Adolf Hoffmeister.

British Library Cataloguing-in-Publication Data
A catalogue record for this book is available from the British
Library.

ISBN 0 8264 8485 9

Printed and bound in Great Britain by MPG Books Ltd,
Bodmin, Cornwall.

CONTENTS

Foreword

by Roger Scruton

In a recent survey of its readers, *Lidové noviny* asked who should be remembered as the greatest Czech of modern times. Karel Čapek came second to T. G. Masaryk, the philosopher who created the First Republic, and who was its first President. Karel Čapek, the playwright, and his brother Josef (a painter) were the leading figures of Czech culture in the brief years of the First Czechoslovak Republic and Karel remains a hero in his homeland. He devoted his life and his talents to the entertainment and instruction of his country-men, and endowed them with an ideal of humane patriotism thanks to which they were able to survive the years of Nazi occupation and Communist insolence, and to re-emerge in our day as a stable and independent nation.

Even today, most Czechs recognize that this ideal of patriotic duty, although imported by Čapek, was made in England. Čapek's *Letters from England* are not merely a masterpiece of Czech prose; they are one of the seminal documents of Central European culture, and among the most influential books of the twentieth century. It is from such a gentle and propaganda-free literature that people can learn how to remain human, in times of public hysteria and private grief. This new translation by Geoffrey Newsome deserves to be as much a classic in the English-speaking world as the original is in Central Europe.

When Čapek wrote these letters, our country was still the metropolitan centre of the largest Empire the world has ever known. Culture and manners were uniform, customs and traditions were intact, and the extraordinary mixture of convention and eccentricity, of law-abidingness and insolence, of charity and snobbery, of sympathy and aloofness had survived the catastrophe of the First World War. To describe this national character was a task for a literary genius. Many made the attempt, but only Čapek really succeeded— succeeded because he saw England from the quite peculiar perspective of the new Czechoslovakia. In describing our country, Čapek was also forging his own.

Čapek's inimitable and witty descriptions are mixed at times with exasperation at the mulish inability of the English to take stock of the outside world. Nevertheless they acknowledge the rare qualities of our national culture—a culture based less on religion than on law, duty and silence. Čapek discerned in the English something of the shrewd resignation and wily self-irony of the Czechs. But he also recognized that, beneath these worldly characteristics, the English were romantic idealists, with a chivalrous streak that rescued them from self-interest.

We can only imagine the life-blow to Karel Čapek when, in 1938 prior to Münich, an Englishman, by renouncing a solemn treaty, betrayed Czechoslovakia to the Nazis. It was perhaps Karel Čapek's good fortune to die of a broken heart on hearing Chamberlain's dismissal of 'a quarrel in a far away country between people of whom we know nothing'. His brother Josef died later in Belsen.

Introduction

by Geoffrey Newsome

In the 1920s and 1930s Karel Čapek was one of the most obvious examples to the world and to his countrymen of the Czechoslovak Republic's emergence as a successful, independent, international nation after centuries of Germanisation and Hapsburg domination. Culturally, the roots of this independence had been laid as early as the last quarter of the eighteenth century and had been nurtured thereafter in the works of such eminent men and women as the philologists, Josef Dobrovský and Josef Jungmann, the historian, František Palacký, the journalist, Karel Havlíček Borovský, the authors, J. K. Tyl, V. K. Klicpera, Božena Němcová, Jan Neruda and Alois Jirásek and the composers, Bedřich Smetana and Antonín Dvořák. Politically, this independence had been won, as almost none of these men and women would ever have dared to have hoped, under the guidance of a remarkable professor of philosophy, Tomáš Garrigue Masaryk, with whom Čapek was to become close friends and of whom he was to write his *Talks with T. G. Masaryk*.

Čapek was twenty-eight when the independent Czechoslovak Republic was established in 1918. Throughout his life therefore he was deeply conscious of Czechoslovak history, of his country's youth and relative immaturity and, in the tradition of his forebears, of his responsibility as a man of letters to the social, intellectual and cultural needs of

3

his country. But his concerns were also more universal; he felt bound not only to speak to and on behalf of the Czechoslovak Republic but to and on behalf of the whole of humanity. Repeatedly and often ingeniously in his writings he alerted man to the dangers to human existence which man himself had created: to the dangers of industrialism, scientific discoveries, human folly, reckless exploitation of the forces of nature and the dictatorship and war which were ultimately to wreck his fledgling nation. Such internationalism was typical of the new Czechoslovak Republic too. Political independence had by and large been won for the Czechs and Slovaks in Britain, France and the United States and Čapek understood, like many others, that the development of his country and perhaps its very survival would depend in part upon its awareness of and close relationship with other countries; and in part, of course, this is what motivated his interest in England, as in other countries like Italy and Spain.

It would be wrong, however, to see Čapek only in the light of his country's tragic history or of his preoccupation with the more tragic potential of mankind. His literary output was prolific and diverse. As a journalist, playwright, novelist, travel writer, essayist, translator, children's writer, poet and short story writer, he explored numerous subjects and a vast array of literary forms. As a man, he was modest, sickly, energetic and popular. Edwin Muir in his autobiography recalls how strangers would greet him in the streets of Prague with a 'Hi, Charlie!' and certainly during his visit to Britain in 1924 he won the instant endearment of the British people. His plays such as *R.U.R.* (from which we derive the word 'robot', a coinage of his brother, Josef), *From the Life of the Insects* and *The Makropulos Affair* were performed with success on many of the world's stages, his novels such as *War with the Newts*, *Hordubal*, *Meteor*, *An Ordinary Life* and other writings were widely translated; and, according to his widow, Olga Scheinpflugová, the Swedish Academy only decided not to nominate him for a Nobel Prize because of the danger in the political climate of the day of nominating an obviously anti-fascist writer.

It may now seem somewhat surprising therefore, having been such a celebrated literary figure, associated with many lastingly famous authors, that Čapek should now be so little known and his works so hard to come by even in his native country. In part, this is due to the cruel and hasty demise of the Czechoslovak Republic, to its Nazi occupation and absorption in the Soviet Bloc, as well as to years of communist censorship and isolation from the West. It is also because Čapek himself died with that Republic, disillusioned like many of his countrymen by the West's betrayal of his country at Münich.

In the years since the Münich Agreement, Nazi occupation and years of communist emasculation, the Czech nation has recovered its political independence. The time has surely also come for Čapek's reputation to be restored.

*

Čapek visited Britain in 1924, thanks largely to another Czechoslovak who was then living in England, Otakar Vočadlo. He had first entered into contact with Vočadlo in October 1921 when he was producer and literary adviser at the Prague theatre, Městké divadlo na Vinohradech. He had been appointed to the post by Jaroslav Kvapil, the librettist of Dvořák's exquisite opera, *Rusalka*, and wrote to Dr.

Dohalský, an acquaintance at the Czechoslovak embassy in London, to ask for details about the latest British plays. Dohalský put Čapek in contact with Vočadlo, who was then a postgraduate at University College, London, and a lengthy correspondence between the two men ensued. For a time, Vočadlo also tried to interest Čapek in P.E.N. ('Poets, Playwrights, Essayists and Novelists') a new, post-war orgaisation which had been founded in London on October 5th, 1921 to further international understanding among authors and editors. Čapek, however, was initially more interested in Vočadlo's news about the British theatre and in his articles about British society and culture for the Czechoslovak newspaper, *Lidové noviny*.

In November 1923, Vočadlo suggested to Marjorie Dawson Scott, the secretary of P.E.N. and daughter of its founder, Catherine Amy Dawson Scott, that she invite Čapek to Britain as P.E.N.'s Guest of Honour. Miss Dawson Scott agreed and Čapek was invited. Čapek, however, delayed in replying. Among his reservations were doubts about his proficiency in English, a fear of London and of travelling in London and a reluctance to forgo the expense of such a visit because he and his brother, Josef, were then building a new house. These reservations were eventually overcome, however, by the combination of an offer from a Czech English scholar, Vilém Mathesius, to accompany Čapek (though Mathesius later had to renege because of an eye disease) and by Čapek's own decision to visit the British Empire Exhibition on behalf of *Lidové noviny*.

These reservations having been overcome, Čapek's first plan was to travel to London after the French premiere of *R.U.R.* That premiere took place earlier than he had expected, however, on April 24th, 1924, and he travelled direct to Britain at the end of May. He arrived in Folkestone on May 28th, very apprehensive, as one may also judge from *Letters from England*, and was met in London by Vočadlo. He stayed in Britain until July 26th.

Čapek began to write *Letters from England* in his first week in Britain, despite countless social engagements. It is unclear when it first occurred to him to write a set of sketches about a tour around Britain but certainly in a letter to Vočadlo on March 23rd, 1924, in which he tried to persuade Vočadlo himself to write some sketches about Britain, it is clear that he had already given considerable thought to what the subject of such sketches might be, as well as to how they might be written. Vočadlo, he urged, should describe London's streets, G. B. Shaw, the stevedores in the ports, student life, the Oxford and Cambridge boat race, the Prince of Wales and G. K. Chesterton: 'in short, visible, lively, interesting things, freely and perhaps philosophically related.' Such were to be the sketches which he himself would shortly write.

These sketches were serialised in *Lidové noviny* from June 15th, 1924, while Čapek was still in Britain, and appeared in book form as *Anglické listy* in October. An English translation was serialised in the *Manchester Guardian* under the title 'How it feels to be in England' from August 1924 and was published in book form in March 1925.

*

The appearance of the word 'England' in the book's title is a misnomer, the sketches really being about parts of the whole of Great Britain. Čapek certainly intended no offence by this. He had, after all, a very deep sympathy for Scotland in particular and recognised several parallels in Scotland's historical position with that of his own country. But, as with many Czechs today, he tended to use 'English' and 'England' as general, if incorrect, approximations for 'British' and 'Britain', as indeed he was to do again in a broadcast for the BBC in 1934 in which he referred to 'this old, paradoxical, particularist, insular, English England, in short, this Great Britain of yours' and in an article for the *Daily Herald* in which he described Edinburgh lawyers as being 'English' (both writings are translated here). That Čapek certainly meant no offence by the book's title is also suggested by the fact that several of his closest acquaintances in Britain were Scottish or Irish, including the London editor of the newspaper in which *Letters from England* was first serialised in Britain, James Bone.

British critical acclaim for Čapek's book in 1925 was unanimous, in Scotland as well as in England. Punch described it as 'the best book about our race since the Germania of Tacitus' and its popularity led to six editions being printed in the first nine months. Not surprisingly, perhaps, the single characteristic which almost all reviewers praised was the book's extraordinary charm. In recent times, charm is a characterisitic which has been much derided. However, the nature of Čapek's charm and the way in which it is created in words are both delightful and instructive. Indeed, for the British reader *Letters from England* may seem more charming than any other adult book which Čapek wrote. In part, this is because Britain itself and Čapek's sense of himself in Britain directly influenced him to the type of charm which he displays in the book. In this sense, it is surely significant that Čapek wrote all of *Letters from England* while he was still in Britain and while he was still experiencing the country. That he was capable of such empathetic identification with the thing he encountered can also be seen in his description of G. B. Shaw, where his style changes and becomes epigrammatic in a way which is quite uncharacteristic in *Letters from England* and which surely reflects the influence of Shaw himself:

> 'He is a vegetarian; I don't know whether from principle or from gourmandaise. One never knows whether people have principles on principle or whether for their own personal satisfaction.'

The greatest part of the charm of *Letters from England* lies in Čapek's own persona and particularly in his vivid sense of himself as an individual who is different from his new surroundings: in particular, as a foreigner from a small country who is visiting a major world power; a foreigner, besides, who speaks little English and is therefore reduced to experiencing Britain in its most direct impressions on him. So it is that at times he seems like a vulnerable, innocent, almost childlike figure, a character who openly admires London's 'Bobbies', is frightened of crossing the street, feels homesick and is respectful to the sheep in Hyde Park. So it is that we witness his childlike licenses of imagination such as conceiving of baskets of old ladies' dried ears at the British Empire Exhibition, or his playful pretences such as of feeling sorry for Marble Arch or wishing that most of London's municipal statues were made of butter. And so it is that his often humorous sense of himself in adverse circumstances reminds us of pre-Victorian British novels as he is hauled along the London underground, pinched by tree roots or shaken about on a London bus 'like an outlandish puppet'.

Čapek's sense of difference from his British surroundings is also charming both because of the modesty and good humour of his comparisons (as, for example, when he compares British farmers and his uncle, a 'Czech peasant farmer', or when he evokes the Czechoslovak people generally, 'manuring the soil on every inch of ground') and because of his enormous pride in his country and optimism for it, both of which qualities, partly thanks to Čapek himself, were typical of the First Republic and which have now been largely replaced among Czechs by a more negative, Hašekian sense of Czech destiny. In particular, Čapek refuses to be discouraged by what he sees in Britain or to feel inferior because of his country's smaller size or population and looks instead to a more intellectual and existential glory:

> 'My homeland which doesn't have a sea, isn't your horizon somewhat narrow and don't you lack the murmur of distant places? Yes, yes, but there can be humming around our heads; if it isn't possible to sail, it is at least possible to think, to furrow the wide and high world with wings of the spirit. I tell you, there is still enough space for expeditions and great ships. Yes, it is necessary to put out to sea continuously; the sea is everywhere where there is courage.'

Such humanistic and existential priorities are typical of Čapek's literary appeal. In *Letters from England* he is largely uninterested in facts, histories and verifiable data and is instead interested in the British people, in their lifestyle, environment and values. It is this humanism which so respects Britain for catering for children and the elderly and which so admires English Literature (his journey around

Britain being largely a personal literary pilgrimage). It is this humanism which is so outraged by aspects of Britain that don't cater for man's personal and social needs, such as the slums of the East End or Britain's streets, or which is bewildered by the Scottish Highlands which reduce him to largely physical description and historical fact. And it is this humanism which explains why his charm shows far less in these bewildered and outraged, Scottish and English chapters than in those in which he employs his particular, instinctive gifts as an artist, his unique fusion of empathy, experience and perception to arrive at an unusual understanding, for example, of the possible influence on British nature of old trees or leather armchairs or to distinguish subtly and categorically between different types of silence.

The greatest appeal of Čapek's charm, however, is his candour. This it is that provokes him to expressions of selfless admiration where he feels that that is due, as well as to expressions of disappointment or despair. Never, for all his playfulness, is his charm evasive or lacking in integrity or fundamentally insincere. Never does he place any importance to himself above the essential honesty of what he feels, with the result that his observations therefore always seem fundamentally just. That he is of course persistently conscious of himself and of a certain ridiculousness in relation to his circumstances in no way detracts from this selfless fairness and indeed specifically contributes to it: by admitting his potential to seem foolish he allows for the inadequacy of his judgements. It is precisely his charm that offers a potentially qualifying balance to his observations.

It may still be surprising, however, that parts of *Letters from England* do not seem more offensive to the British reader than they do. Čapek, after all, is often highly critical

11

of what he sees. Again, one reason for our not being offended is a recognition of the very humanism which informs all of Čapek's observations. Throughout *Letters from England* we are conscious that while he is of course visiting the local and specific, his overwhelming interest and inquiry are nevertheless humanistic and existential. Throughout, we are conscious that he is not simply visiting Britain but another of mankind's experiments and habitats and is not simply asking, What is Britain? and, Who are the British?, but, What is man as I find him here? and, What lessons can I learn from and for his life here? As profoundly as we necessarily bear some of his criticisms of Britain, therefore, (when he *is* being critical) we are never inclined to view these as being merely petty or nationalistic.

So manifold are Čapek's charms that there are still many more for the reader to discover which I have not mentioned. There is, however, at least one other aspect of *Letters from England* which no even brief introduction should ignore and that is in regard to *Letters from England* as a textual achievement. At the risk of stating the obvious, *Letters from England* would possess no charm at all if it were not for the charm which Čapek has created in his text; and, less obviously, this charm, as he has chosen to create his text, also at times becomes formally necessary. There are many verbal ways in which Čapek creates this charm. These include his personal interjections and direct appeals to the reader such as 'I tell you', 'God help me' and 'Well then', or his often understated descriptions of places and people as being 'very nice', 'very good' or even 'kind and nice'. His descriptions are often charming by being poetic and his sentences, paragraphs and chapters are often poetically judged in their balance, movement and completion. He frequently uses language in an impressionistic way to create his own persona, as in the short, vulnerable, childlike clauses in 'Hyde Park':

'A little man stands in the middle with a baton, gives an A, and the whole group sings, even very respectably and polyphonically. I only wanted to listen in silence because I don't belong to this parish, but my neighbour, a gentleman in a top hat, urged me to sing too and I sang aloud and glorified the Lord without words and without a tune.'

or else he toys with words and phrases playfully: 'If we also touch briefly on its underground railway station we have exhausted everything, including our patience.'

Such textual devices both create in themselves and support the notion of Čapek's charm. But, as I have suggested, often these devices are also formally necessary. Often what is consistent with Čapek's notional charm is in fact a device required by the choices which he has made for his text. Among these are such fundamental decisions as about the level of his engagement with the perceived, the degree of his commitment to his opinions and observations and the temper of his expression; and among his textual devices are his claims to have confused or forgotten what he has seen, or his decisions not to expound in detail on what he has observed or thought because he needs to move on. Ultimately, these decisions and devices create the whole charm of *Letters from England* and they are brought together by Čapek's exceptional ingenuousness.

Translator's note

The first translator of *Anglické listy* into English was Čapek's first translator in Britain, Paul Selver. Prior to translating works by Čapek, Selver had translated a book of Czech poetry and had become translator to the Czechoslovak legation in London after the First World War. By Vočadlo's account, however, which is supported by some of Čapek's correspondence, the relationship with Selver was to be one which both he and the far longer suffering Čapek would soon regret.

According to Vočadlo, Selver frequently neglected to send Čapek cuttings of serialised translations, did not send Čapek translations in book form and even failed to notify Čapek that translations existed in book form at all. Between 1925 and 1926 he apparently prevented a promising London premiere of *The Makropulos Affair* starring Edith Evans because he was late in translating the play (he was writing a novel of his own) and because he then insisted on translating the play himself when it was offered to (and begun by) another translator, Laurence Hyde. By the time that Selver had finally translated the play, Edith Evans was no longer available and Nigel Playfair, who had been interested in producing it, decided that the timing was no longer suitable for English

audiences. Between 1926 and 1927 Selver apparently adver-
tised himself in the British press as the 'author of *R.U.R.*', an
audacity which Čapek believed could only have been a joke,
and in 1928 his excessive demands and interference were
judged to have contributed to the loss of a lucrative contract
to film Čapek's plays in America. 'Selver,' Čapek told Vočadlo,
'has cost me 360,000' (Czechoslovak Crowns); and on his
visit to Britain that year, Čapek did not want to see Selver.

Selver's translation of *Anglické listy* caused Čapek anxiety too. In addition to not sending Čapek newspaper cuttings
of and about the serialised translation, Selver offered the
complete translation to a small publisher without consulting
Čapek's London and Prague agents and without adequately
settling the matters of Čapek's contract and fee. In a letter in
June 1925 Čapek wrote in frustration to Vočadlo that he had
received neither a contract nor copies of his book and that
he had received instead £20 from the publisher for an
unspecified number of books. 'But Mr. Selver,' he regretted,
'always did want to act as though, as translator, he had lim-
itless authority.'

Just as disappointing was the standard of some of
Selver's translation. The number of literal mistakes alone is
surprising, some of which Čapek noticed himself, but
Vočadlo also claims that even when Selver had been notified
of some of these mistakes, he failed to correct them. From the
very first line of his *Letters from England* Selver omitted parts
of Čapek's text and bowdlerised it extensively. The serious-
ness of this was amplified by the fact that English translations often formed the basis of translations into other
languages.

It was principally these shortcomings of the original
translation and the fact that it has been out of print a long

time that persuaded me to try a new translation of my own. For this translation I have corrected a large number of Čapek's transcriptions of British place-names, have repositioned his drawings so that they bear a more direct relation to the text and have allowed for a slight formal separation of the chapter 'The Lake District' from the chapters on Scotland so as to avoid confusion or Selver's solution of re-locating the chapter. I have also translated two related pieces of writing by Čapek, both because they appear in later Czech editions of *Anglické listy* and because they provide an additional record of Čapek's and even the Czechoslovak Republic's relation to Britain.

The only persistent uncertainty I have had in translating this book has been whether or not to use contractions. Finally, I have decided in most cases to use contractions in negative structures and not in others. In this way, I hope that my translation most closely evokes Čapek's own, deliberate blend of formality and informality, self-consciousness and artlessness. I have avoided contractions for his newspaper article but for his radio broadcast I have used all possible contractions, as befits the different forms. I hope that the inclusion of these two documents will provide an instructive source of contrast to *Letters from England*, in as far as the formal, literary qualities of *Letters from England* are so complete and so well-judged that one may perhaps only become fully aware of them in contrast to other works, even when those works have been written by Čapek himself.

Geoffrey Newsome
Bishop's Cleeve
2000

A Chronology of Karel Čapek

1890	9th January: Birth of Karel Čapek in Malé Svatoňovice, Bohemia.
1895	Begins school in Úpice.
1901-5	Studies at Gymnázium (academic secondary school) in Hradec Králové. Is expelled for belonging to a patriotic student society.
1904	Publishes first poem.
1905	Studies at Gymnázium in Brno.
1907	Family moves to Prague. Studies at Gymnázium in Prague.
1909	Begins studies in Philosophy at Charles University, Prague.
1910	Studies at Friedrich Wilhelm University, Berlin.
1911	Studies at the Sorbonne, Paris. Begins to write *Loupežník* (*The Brigand*) with brother, Josef (b. 1887).
1915	Becomes Doctor of Philosophy from Charles University, Prague.
1916	Publishes first book, *Zářivé hlubiny* (*The Shining Depths*), which includes the play *Lásky hra osudná* (*Love's Fateful Game*), written with Josef.
1917	Becomes a member of the editorial staff of the weekly, *Národ*.

	Publishes a collection of short stories, *Boží muka* (*The Wayside Cross*). Joins the editorial staff of the newspaper, *Národní listy*.
1918	Publishes *Pragmatismus čili Filozofie praktického života* (*Pragmatism or the Philosophy of the Practical Life*). Publishes *Krakonošova zahrada* (*The Garden of Krakonoš*), a collection of prose writings written with Josef.
1919	Translation of poetry by Apollinaire.
1920	*Loupežník* (*The Brigand*) premieres at the National Theatre, Prague. Meets Olga Scheinpflugová, the daughter of a colleague at *Národní listy*. Publishes a collection of articles, *Kritika slov* (*A Critique of Words*), and a play, *R.U.R.*
1921	*R.U.R.* premieres in Hradec Králové and later at the National Theatre, Prague. Publishes *Trapné povídky* (*Awkward Tales*). Joins the editorial staff of the newspaper, *Lidové noviny*, with Josef. Becomes a producer at the Prague theatre, *Městské divadlo Královských Vinohrad*. Publishes the play, *Ze života hmyzu* (*From the Life of Insects*), written with Josef.
1922	*Ze života hmyzu* (*From the Life of Insects*) premieres at the National Theatre, Brno and later at the National Theatre, Prague. Meets President T. G. Masaryk for the first time when

Masaryk visits the Vinohrady theatre.
Publishes a novel, *Továrna na Absolutno* (*A Factory for the Absolute*). *Věc Makropulos* (*The Makropulos Affair*) premieres at the Vinohrady theatre.

1923   *Ze života hmyzu* (*From the Life of Insects*) premieres in Berlin. Čapek travels in Germany. Leaves his post at the Vinohrady theatre. Travels to Italy. Publishes *Italské listy* (*Letters from Italy*).

1924   Čapek's mother dies. Publishes a novel, *Krakatit*. Travels to Britain. Publishes *Anglické listy* (*Letters from England*).

1925   Is nominated Chairman of the new Prague P.E.N. Publishes *Jak vzniká divadelní hra* (*How a Play Comes into Being*). Publishes collection of articles, *O nejbližších věcech* (*On Intimate Things*).

1927   *Adam Stvořitel* (*Adam the Creator*) premieres at the National Theatre, Prague. Publishes *Skandální aféra Josefa Holouška* (*The Disgraceful Scandal of Josef Holoušek*).

1928   Publishes first part of *Hovory s T. G. Masarykem* (*Talks with T. G. Masaryk*).

1929   Publishes *Povídky z jedné kapsy* (*Tales from One Pocket*). Publishes *Zahradníkův rok* (*The Gardener's Year*). Čapek's father dies. Travels to Spain. Publishes *Povídky z druhé kapsy*

(*Tales from the Other Pocket*).

1930	Publishes *Výlet do Španěl* (*A Trip to Hispania*).
1931	Publishes second part of *Hovory s T. G. Masarykem* (*Talks with T. G. Masaryk*). Travels in Holland. Publishes collection of literary essays, *Marsyas čili Na okraj literatury* (*Marsyas or To the Margins of Literature*). Publishes *Devatero pohádek* (*Nine Fairy Tales*).
1932	Publishes *Apokryfy* (*Apocryphal Stories*). Publishes *O věcech obecných čili Zóon politikon* (*On Common Things or Zoon Politikon*). Publishes *Obrázky z Holandska* (*Pictures from Holland*). Publishes *Dášeňka čili Život štěněte* (*Dashenyka or The Life of a Puppy*).
1933	Publishes first part of a novel trilogy, *Hordubal*. Resigns as Chairman of P.E.N.
1934	Publishes second part of the trilogy, *Povětroň* (*Meteor*). Publishes third part of the trilogy, *Obyčejný život* (*An Ordinary Life*).
1935	Publishes third part of *Hovory s T. G. Masarykem* (*Talks with T. G. Masaryk*). Travels in the Dolomites with Olga Scheinpflugová. Marries Olga Scheinpflugová.
1936	Publishes novel, *Válka s Mloky* (*War with the Newts*). Travels through Denmark, Sweden and Norway. The Norwegian press propose Čapek for the Nobel Prize for Literature. Publishes *Cesta na sever* (*A Journey to the North*).

Publishes *Jak se dělají noviny* (*How Newspapers Are Made*).

1937   *Bílá nemoc* (*The White Sickness*) premieres at the Estates Theatre, Prague and then at the State Theatre, Brno. Travels through Austria, Switzerland and southern France. President Masaryk dies. Publishes novel, *První parta* (*The First Crew*).

1938   *Matka* (*Mother*) premieres at the Estates Theatre, Prague. 25th December (6.45pm): Čapek dies. Leaves an unfinished novel, *Život a dílo skladatele Foltýna*, (*The Life and Work of the Composer, Foltýn*).

Drawing of Karel Čapek by Adolf Hoffmeister, 1938

1939   Josef Čapek incarcerated at Dachau concentration camp.

1945   Josef dies in Bergen-Belsen concentration camp.

1968   Olga Scheinpflugová dies.

ENGLAND

FIRST IMPRESSIONS

'One must begin from the beginning,' the master, Chauliac, once advised me; but since I have already been on this Babylonian island ten days, I have lost the beginning. With what should I begin now? With grilled bacon or the exhibition at Wembley? With Mr. Shaw or London policemen? I see that I am beginning very confusedly; but as for those policemen, I must say that they are recruited according to their beauty and size; they are like gods, a head above mortal men, and their power is unlimited. When one of those two-metre Bobbies at Piccadilly raises his arm, all vehicles come to a halt, Saturn becomes fixed and Uranus stands still on his heavenly orbit, waiting until Bobby lowers his arm again. I have never seen anything so superhuman.

The greatest surprise for any traveller is when he finds something in a foreign country which he has read about a hundred times or seen a hundred times in pictures. I was astonished when I found Milan Cathedral in Milan or the Colosseum in Rome. It is a somewhat ghastly impression because you have the feeling that you have already been there at some time or that you have already experienced it once, perhaps in a dream or something. It takes you aback to find that in Holland there really are windmills and canals or that on the Strand in London there really are so many people that it makes you feel unwell. There are two absolutely fantastic impressions: to discover something unexpected and to discover something very familiar. One always expresses amazement when one meets an old acquaintance out of the blue. Well then, I was similarly amazed when I found the Houses of Parliament on the river Thames, gentlemen in grey top hats in the streets, two-metre-tall Bobbies at the crossroads, and so on. It was a surprise to discover that England really is English.

But so that I really begin at the beginning, I have drawn you a picture of what England looks like when you approach it from the Channel. The white parts are simply cliffs and above them grows grass. True, it is all

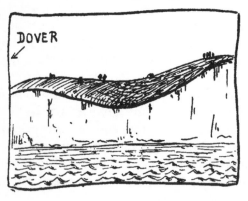

built quite solidly enough, one might almost say on rock, but to have a continent beneath one's feet makes one feel more secure.

I have also drawn you a picture of Folkestone, which is where I landed. In the sunset it looked like a castle with crenellations; later, however, it became clear that these were only chimneys.

Once I had set foot on land I found to my surprise that I didn't speak or understand a single word of English. So I hid away in the nearest train. Fortunately, it turned out that it was going to London. During the journey I discovered that what I had considered to be England is in fact only one great, English park, nothing but meadows and pastures, exquisite trees, century-old lanes and here and there, sheep, just as in Hyde Park, and obviously for the improvement of your impression. While I was still in Holland I saw people with their rears exposed to the skies, working with their hands in the earth. In England one sees red bungalows, a girl waving over a hedge or a cyclist bicycling along a lane. Otherwise, people are surprisingly scarce. A person from our country is used to seeing someone manuring the soil on every inch of ground.

At last, the train bores its way through some strange sorts of houses. There are a hundred of them, completely identical; then a whole street the same; then again and again. It gives one an impression of frantic multiplication. The train flies past a whole town which has some terrible curse hanging over it because every house, out of whatever desperate necessity, has two pillars beside the door. The next block lies under the spell of having nothing but iron balconies. The following block is forever condemned to having grey bricks. Gloomy, irreversible fate has determined that the next street shall have blue verandas. Then there is a whole quarter which, because of some unknown wrong, has been inflicted with having five steps at every door. It would relieve me no end if one house had only three but for whatever reason this isn't possible. And the next street is completely red.

Later, I got off the train, fell into the arms of a good, Czech, guardian angel and was led to left and right, up and down. I tell you, it was awful. They loaded me onto a train and took me out at Surbiton, cheered me up, fed me and put me into a feather bed. It was as dark there as at home and the dreams I had were all-embracing: something about the boat, something about Prague and something strange which I have already forgotten.

Thank God that I didn't have fifty dreams all the same, one after the other. Praise Heaven that at least dreams aren't produced wholesale like London's streets.

THE ENGLISH PARK

The trees are perhaps the most beautiful things in England. The meadows too of course and the police-men, but mainly the trees, the beautifully broad-backed, old, ample, free, venerable and huge trees. The

trees in Hampton Court, Richmond Park, Windsor and I don't know where else. Maybe these trees have a large influence on Toryism in England. I think that they preserve aristocratic instincts, historical precedent, conservatism, protectionism, golf, the House of Lords and other old and peculiar things. Perhaps I would be an ardent Labourite if I lived in the Street of Iron Balconies or the Street of Grey Bricks but seated under an oak tree in Hampton Park I felt a risky inclination to acknowledge the worth of old things, the higher mission of old trees, the harmonious branching out of tradition and a respect for everything which is strong enough to preserve itself throughout the ages.

It seems that in England there are a lot of these ancient trees. In almost everything that one encounters here, in the gentlemen's clubs, in literature and in households there is a feel of timber and ancient leaves, of reverend and frightfully solid trees. Here, in fact, one never sees anything spectacularly new; only the underground is new, which is perhaps why it is so ugly. But old trees and old things possess sprites and exotic, waggish spirits. The English possess these sprites too. They are immensely serious, solid and venerable; suddenly something somehow crackles in them, they say something grotesque, a morsel of impish humour shoots out of them and once again they look as serious as an old, leather chair. Perhaps they are made of old wood.

I don't even know why, but this sober England strikes me as being the most fabulous and romantic of all the countries I have ever seen. Perhaps it is because of these old trees. Or not: perhaps it is because of the lawns. It is because here people walk across the meadows instead of on the paths. We others dare only walk on paths and footpaths. This undoubtedly has a huge influence on our spiritual life. When I saw my first gentleman roaming across a lawn at Hampton Court I thought that he was some fairy-tale figure, except that he was wearing a top hat. I expected him to ride to Kingston on a stag or to begin dancing or some gardener to come after him and scold him bitterly. But nothing happened. Finally, even I found the courage to set off straight across the meadow to the oak tree which stands at the beginning of this letter in a beautiful pasture. Again nothing happened; but I have never had a feeling of such boundless freedom as at that moment. It is very odd: here obviously man isn't thought of as a verminous beast. Here there is no gloomy opinion of him that the grass won't grow beneath his hooves. Here it is his prerogative to cross a meadow as if he were a water nymph or lord of the manor. I think that this has a marked influence on his nature and view of the world. It opens up the miraculous possibility of going another way than by the path and in doing so of not having to consider oneself vermin, a lout or an anarchist.

I reflected on all of this under an oak tree in Hampton Park but ultimately even old roots begin to pinch. I am sending you a small picture at least of what an English park looks like. I also wanted to draw in a stag but I admit that I couldn't manage it from memory.

LONDON STREETS

As far as London itself is concerned, it reeks in general of petrol, burnt grass and tallow, differently from Paris, where in addition there is the stench of cosmetic powder, coffee and cheese. In Prague every street smells differently; in this respect there is nothing better than Prague. More complicated are the voices of London. There at the heart, on the Strand or in Piccadilly, it sounds, folks, like a spinning mill with thousands of spindles. It rattles, rumbles, purrs, gurgles and bubbles with thousands of packed motor vehicles, buses, cars and steam engines; and you sit on top of a bus which cannot move forward and which rattles idly, are shaken about by its rumbling and jump about in your seat like an outlandish, stuffed puppet. Then there are the side streets, gardens, squares, roads, groves and crescents, up to this miserable road in Notting Hill where I am writing this: all sorts of Streets of Two Columns, Streets of the Same Railings, Streets of the Seven Steps In Front of Each House, and so on. Well then, here some desperate variations on the sound of 'i' announce the milkman, a lamenting 'yeyey' means simply kindling wood, 'oowoh' is the coalman's war cry and the horrendous din of a delirious sailor reports that some youth is selling five cabbage heads from a child's pram. And at night the cats make love as wildly as on the roofs of Palermo, despite all tales of English puritanism. Only the people are quieter here than elsewhere; they speak to each other out of the sides of their mouths and look to see if they are home yet. And that is the most bizarre thing in the English streets: here you don't see venerable ladies chatting on the corner about what happened at the Smiths' or the Greens' or lovers wandering aimlessly like sleep-walkers, arm-in-arm, or honourable citizens sitting in front of their houses with their hands on their knees (by the way, I still haven't seen a cabinet maker here or a locksmith or workshops or a journeyman or an apprentice; here there are only shops, nothing but shops, nothing but Westminster Bank and Midland Bank Ltd.), or men drinking in the street or benches in the market-place or loiterers or layabouts or maid-servants or old-age pensioners; in short, nothing, nothing, nothing. A London street is just a type of trough which life flows through in order to get home. People don't live in the streets, gaze, speak, stand or sit; the streets are just for passing through. Here the street isn't the most interesting saloon where you encounter a thousand spectacles or have a thousand adventures speak to you, a saloon where people whistle or fight, make a racket, flirt, rest, write poetry

or philosophise, relieve themselves and enjoy life and make jokes and discuss politics and cluster in pairs, in threes, in families, in crowds or in revolutions. In our country, in Italy and in France a street is a sort of great pub or public gardens, a village green, a meeting place, a playing field and a theatre, an extended home and a threshold. Here it is something which doesn't belong to anyone and doesn't bring anyone closer to other people. Here one doesn't meet people and things; here one only passes them by.

A person in our country sticks his head out of the window and he is already in the street. But an English home isn't only separated from the street by a lace curtain but by a small garden and railings, by ivy, a small lawn with a hedge, a door-knocker and long-standing tradition. The English home must have its own small garden because the street isn't a mad and delightful garden for it; in the garden it must have its own swing or play area because the street isn't a play area or slide for it. The poetry of the English home is bought at the expense of the English street being so unpoetic. And revolutionary mobs will never line the streets here because these streets are too long for that. And too monotonous.

It is a comfort that there are buses here, ships of the desert, camels bearing you on their backs through the brick immensity of London. It puzzles me that they don't lose their way although they aren't mostly steered by the sun or stars, owing to the cloudiness of the region. I don't yet know by what secret signs the driver distinguishes Ladbroke Grove from Great Western Road or Kensington Park Street. I don't know why he prefers to drive off to East Acton instead of going to Pimlico or Hammersmith. Everything after all is so curiously the same that I don't understand why he actually specialises in East Acton. Maybe his home is there, one of the ones with two columns and seven steps by the door. These houses look a little like family tombs. I tried to draw them but, try as I might, I couldn't achieve a sufficiently hopeless appearance. Besides this, I haven't got any grey paint with me to paint them in.

Not to forget: of course, I went to have a look at Baker Street and I came back terribly disappointed. There isn't even a trace of Sherlock Holmes there; it is a business thoroughfare of peerless respectability which has no higher goal than to lead into Regent's Park, which, after long endeavours, it almost manages to do. If we also touch briefly on its underground railway station we have exhausted everything, including our patience.

TRAFFIC

But not as long as I live will I become reconciled to what is known here as 'traffic', that is, to the volume of traffic in the streets. I remember with horror the day when they first brought me to London. First, they took me by train, then they ran through some huge, glass halls and pushed me into a barred cage which looked like a scales for weighing cattle. This was 'a lift' and it descended through an armour-plated well, whereupon they hauled me out and slid away through serpentine, underground corridors. It was like a horrible dream. Then there was a sort of tunnel or sewer with rails, and a buzzing train flew in. They threw me into it and the train flew on and it was very musty and oppressive in there, obviously because of the proximity to hell. Whereupon they took me out again and ran through new catacombs to an escalator which rattles like a mill and hurtles to the top with people on it. I tell you, it is like a fever. Then there were several more corridors and stairways and despite my resistance they led me out into the street, where my heart sank. A fourfold line of vehicles shunts along without end or interruption;

buses, chugging mastodons tearing along in herds with bevies of little people on their backs, delivery vans, lorries, a flying pack of cars, steam engines, people running, tractors, ambulances, people climbing up onto the roofs of buses like squirrels, a new herd of motorised elephants; there, and now everything stands still, a muttering and rattling stream, and it can't go any further; but even I can't go any further, remembering the horror which the idea awoke in me that I would have to cross to the other side of the street. I managed with a certain degree of success and from that time on I have crossed London's streets countless times; but as long as I live I shall never become reconciled to it.

Then I returned from London, broken-hearted, desperate, struck down in spirit and in body. For the first time in my life I felt a blind and furious opposition to modern civilisation. It seemed to me that there is something barbaric and disastrous in this terrible hoarding of people. Apparently there are seven and a half million of them, but I didn't count. I only know that my first impression of this great mass was almost tragic; it made me feel anxious and I longed infinitely for Prague, just as when a small child gets lost in the woods. Yes, I freely admit it, I was scared; I was scared of getting lost, of my bus not coming, of something happening to me, of my being damned, of human life having no worth, of man being a hypertrophied bacterium teeming in the millions on a sort of mildewy potato, of it all being perhaps only a sickening dream, of humanity dying out through some awful disaster, of man being powerless, of my bursting into tears for no reason whatsoever and of everyone laughing at me: all seven and a half million of them. Perhaps sometime later I will understand what at first sight so frightened me and inspired my infinite anguish. But, all well and good, today I am a little more accustomed to it, I walk, run, swerve, travel, climb onto the roofs of buses or tear around in lifts and tubes just like anyone else, but only at one price: that I am not allowed to think about it. As soon as I want to acknowledge what is going on around me I have the same torturous feeling of something bad, monstrous and disastrous for which I know no solace. And then, you know, I feel unbearably lonely.

And sometimes everything stops for about half an hour, for the simple reason that there is too much of it. Sometimes at Charing Cross a knot forms and before they disentangle it vehicles extend from the Bank up until somewhere after Brompton Road; and in the meantime you sit in your vehicle and think about how it is going to look in twenty years' time. Since such congestion builds up all too often, a lot of people think about this. It hasn't yet been resolved whether people will walk over roofs or underground; it is only certain that it is already impossible to use the earth, which is a remarkable achievement of modern civilisation. As for me, I prefer the earth, like the giant, Antaeus. I have drawn you a small picture, but in reality it seems even worse because it roars like a factory. However, drivers don't hoot their horns like lunatics and people by no means swear at each other; they are after all a tranquil people.

TRAFFIC

Meanwhile, I have deciphered that, among other things, the mad cry of 'oh-ay-oh' in the street signifies potatoes, 'oy' is oil and 'oo-ooh' is a bottle of something mysterious. And sometimes a whole band sets up on the kerb of the largest street and plays, blows into trumpets, beats drums and collects pennies; or an Italian tenor steps up in front of the windows and sings *Rigoletto*, *Il Trovatore* or a fiery song of longing, 'I've been done', just as in Naples. However, I have met only one person who whistled; it was on Cromwell Road and he was black.

HYDE PARK

And when I was at my saddest in this English land—
it being an English Sunday, plagued with unspeakable
boredom—, I set off along Oxford Street. I simply
wanted to go eastwards to be nearer to my homeland
but I went in the wrong direction and wandered due
west and so ended up in Hyde Park. It is called Marble
Arch there because there is a marble archway which
leads nowhere. In fact, I don't know why it stands
there. I felt somewhat sorry for it and went to have a
look and while I was there I saw something and ran
over to take a look at it because there were hosts of
people there. And when I understood what was going
on I instantly felt more cheerful.

It is a large, open space and anyone who chooses
can bring a chair or a platform or nothing at all and
can begin to speak. After a while, five or twenty or three
hundred people listen to him, answer him, contradict,
nod their heads and sometimes sing pious and secular
hymns with the speaker. Sometimes an opponent wins
the people over to his side and takes up the word
himself. Sometimes a crowd separates by simple

fission or a coup, like the lowest organisms and cell colonies. Some clusters have a firm and enduring consistency, others continuously disintegrate and spill over, grow, swell, multiply or disperse. The larger churches have small, mobile pulpits but most speakers simply stand on the ground, suck at a wet cigarette and preach about vegetarianism, the Lord God, education, reparations or spiritualism. Never in my life have I seen anything like it.

Since, sinner that I am, I hadn't been to any preaching for many years, I went to listen. Out of modesty, I tagged onto a small, quiet group. A young, hunch-backed man with beautiful eyes was speaking there, evidently a Polish Jew. After a long time I understood that his subject was only education and I went over to a large crowd where an elderly gentleman in a top hat was bobbing about in a pulpit. I discovered that he was representing some Hyde Park Mission. He threw his arms about in such a manner that I was frightened that he would fly over the handrail. Another group was being preached to by an elderly lady. I am not in the least against female emancipation but, in short, a person, you know, cannot listen to the female voice. A woman is congenitally handicapped from public life by her organs (I mean her vocal organs). When a woman gives a speech I always have the feeling that I am a little boy and that my mother is scolding me. I didn't quite understand why the lady with the pince-nez was scolding me. I only know that she was shouting that we should examine our souls. In the next crowd a Catholic was preaching in front of a high crucifix. For the first time in my life I saw the promulgation of the faith to heretics. It was very nice and it finished in song, for which I tried to sing a second part; unfortunately, I didn't know the tune. Several groups devoted themselves exclusively to song. A little man stands in the middle with a baton, gives an A, and the whole group sings, even very respectably and poly-phonically. I only wanted to listen in silence because I don't belong to this parish, but my neighbour, a gentleman in a top hat, urged me to sing too and I sang aloud and glorified the Lord without words and with-out a tune. An amorous couple comes along, the young man removes his cigarette from his mouth and sings, the girl sings too, an old lord sings and a youth with a bat under his arm, and a threadbare little man in the middle of the circle conducts graciously, as if at the Grand Opera. Nothing until that time had pleased me half as much here. I sang again with two other churches and listened to some preaching about Socialism and the tidings of some Metropolitan Secular Society. I stood a while next to some tiny debating groups. One unusually ragged gentleman championed conservative social principles but he spoke such awful Cockney that I couldn't understand him at all. His adversary was an evolutionary Socialist who was to all appearances a better sort of bank clerk. Another group had only five members. There was a brown Indian, a one-eyed man in a flat cap, a fat, Armenian Jew and two other, taciturn men with pipes. The one-eyed man insisted with frightful pessimism that 'something is sometimes nothing', whereas the Indian championed the more cheerful view that 'something is always something', which he repeated twenty times in rather poor English. Then an old grandfather took up his place. He had a long cross in his hand and on it a standard with the sign, 'Thy Lord calleth thee'. He said something in a weak, husky voice but no-one listened to him so I, a lost foreigner, stopped and served him as a listener. Afterwards, I wanted to go on my way because it was already dark, but some anxious person stopped me and I don't know what he said. I replied that I was a foreigner, that London was a terrible affair but that I liked the English, that I had already seen something of the

world but that little had pleased me as much as the speakers in Hyde Park. Before I had told him everything, about ten people had begun standing around us, quietly listening. I could have tried to found a new church but no sufficiently watertight article of faith occurred to me and besides that I don't speak English well enough, so I slipped away.

Beyond the railings at Hyde Park some sheep were grazing; and when I looked at them, one, obviously the eldest, stood up and started bleating. I listened to his sheepy preaching and only when he had said his fill did I go home, satisfied and purified as if after divine service. I could follow up on this with excellent reflections on democracy, the English character, the need for faith and other things; but I would rather leave the whole episode to its natural beauty.

AT THE NATURAL
HISTORY MUSEUM

'Have you been to the British Museum?'
'Have you seen the Wallace Collection?'
'Have you been to the Tate Gallery yet?'
'Have you had a look at the South Kensington Museum?'
'Have you been to the National Gallery?'

Yes, yes, yes; I have been everywhere. But now allow me to sit down and speak of something else. What did I want to say? Yes, strange and great is Nature; and I, a tireless pilgrim of pictures and statues, admit that the conches and crystals in the Natural History Museum gave me the greatest delight. Of course, the mammoths and saurians are very beautiful too; likewise the fish, butterflies, antelopes and other beasts of the field; but the prettiest are the conches and shells because they look as if a divine, playful spirit had created them for his own amusement, bewitched by innumerable possibilities. They are pink, fleshy like a girl's mouth, purple, amber, pearl and black, white and speckled, as heavy as an anvil and as diminutive as Queen Mab's powder compact, twirled, grooved, prickly, oval, similar to kidneys, eyes, lips, arrows, helmets and nothing on earth, translucent, opalescent, delicate, terrible and indescribable. What did I want to say? Yes, when I was looking over the treasures and caskets of art, the collections of furniture, the weapons, clothing, carpets, carvings and porcelain, things that were wrought, engraved, woven, kneaded, hammered, lined and painted, glazed and embroidered and knitted, I saw anew: strange and great is Nature. All of these are different types of shell, sweated out by a strange, divine and urgent playfulness. A wet, naked slug gave birth to all of this, shaking with creative madness. Magnificent little thing, netsuke from Japan or eastern fabric; if I could keep you at home, what you would mean to me! A human secret, the manifestation of man, a graceful, foreign tongue. But in this frightful and immeasurable stockpiling there are no longer individuals, a personal touch or history; there is only lunatic Nature, animal creativity, a fantastic abundance of beautiful, bizarre shells fished out of the timeless ocean. So, be like Nature; create; create things which are bizarre, beautiful, grooved or twisted, bright and translucent; the more abundantly, strangely and purely you create the nearer you will be to Nature or perhaps to God. Nature is great.

But I mustn't forget the crystals, their shapes, laws and colours. There are crystals like cathedral pillars, as delicate as mildew and as sharp as needles, crystals which are limpid, blue, green like nothing on earth, fiery-coloured or black, mathematical, perfect, similar to the designs of strange, deranged scholars or reminiscent of livers, hearts, huge sexual organs and animal phlegm. They are crystal caves or monstrous bubbles of mineral dough. There is mineral fermentation, melting, growth, architecture and engineering. I swear to God, a Gothic church is not the most complicated of crystals. Even in us a crystalline strength persists. Egypt crystallised into pyramids and obelisks, Greece into columns, Gothic into pinnacles and London into cubes of black mud. Innumerable

laws of construction and composition run through matter like secret, mathematical flashes of lightning. We must be exact, mathematical and geometric to be equal to Nature. Number and fantasy, law and abundance are the feverish forces of Nature. Becoming a part of Nature doesn't mean sitting under a green tree but creating crystals and ideas, creating laws and shapes, breaking into matter with incandescent flashes of lightning of a divine calculation.

Ah, how insufficiently exotic, how insufficiently courageous and exact is poetry!

OUR PILGRIM SIFTS THROUGH OTHER MUSEUMS

Wealthy England has assembled the treasures of the whole world in her collections. None too creative herself, she has carted off metope from the Acropolis and Egyptian porphyry or granite colossi, Assyrian relief boulders, knotty, ornamental pieces from ancient Yucatan, smiling Buddhas, Japanese carvings and lacquers, the flower of Continental art and a welter of colonial monuments, iron mountings, fabrics, glass-work, vases, snuff boxes, book bindings, statues, pictures, enamel, inlaid escritoires, Saracen sabres and, God help me, I don't know what else: perhaps everything that has some value in the world.

Of course, I should now be very enlightened about various styles and cultures. I should say something about stages in the development of art. I should mentally classify and separate all this material which is exhibited here for our amazement and enlightenment. However, instead of this I have torn my garb and I ask myself: Where is the perfection of man? Well, it is terrible, but it is everywhere. My word, it is a ghastly discovery to find the perfection of man even at the

outset of his being, to find it in the fashioning of the
first stone arrow, to find it in a barbarian's drawing, to
find it in China, in Fiji and in ancient Nineveh and
everywhere where man has left a memorial of his
creative life. I have seen so many things and I could
have chosen. Very well, I tell you then that I don't know

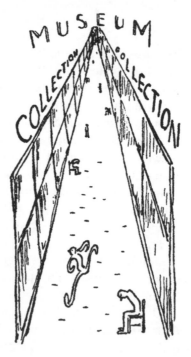

whether man is more perfect, loftier and more
attractive creating the first urn or ornamenting a celebrated Portland vase. I don't know whether it is more

50

perfect to be a cave-man or a Briton from the West End. I don't know whether it is a higher and more godly art to paint a portrait of Queen Victoria on canvas or a portrait of a penguin with one's fingers in the air, the way that the natives of Tierra del Fuego do. I tell you, it is terrible; terrible is the relativity of time and space, but more terrible still is the relativity of culture and history. Nowhere either behind us or in front of us is there a point of tranquillity, of the ideal, of man's completion and perfection, because it is everywhere and nowhere and every place in space and time where man has set up his work is unsurpassable. And I don't even know now whether a portrait by Rembrandt is more perfect than a dance mask from the Gold Coast. I have seen too much. We too must equal Rembrandt or a mask from the Gold or Ivory Coast; there is no progress, no 'up' or 'down'; there is only endlessly new creativity. This is the only example which history, cultures, collections and the whole world's treasures give us: create like madmen, create unceasingly, in this place and at this moment one should create the peak and perfection of human achievement, one must ascend as high as fifty thousand years ago or as in a Gothic Madonna or in that stormy landscape over there by Constable. If there are ten thousand traditions there is no tradition at all. It isn't possible to choose something from complete abundance. It is only possible to add something new.

If you look in the London collections for ivory carvings or embroidered tobacco pouches, you will find them. If you look for the perfection of human achievement you will find it in the Indian museum and the Babylonian gallery, in the Daumiers, Turners, Watteaus and the Elgin marbles. But then you leave this accumulation of the whole world's treasures and you can travel for hours and miles on top of a bus, from Ealing to East Ham and from Clapham up to Bethnal Green, and you will find hardly any human achievement that will please you with its beauty and luxuriance. Art is what is stored behind glass in galleries, museums and the rooms of rich people; but it doesn't run about in the streets here, it doesn't twinkle with pretty window ledges, it isn't stationed on the corner like a monument, it doesn't greet you with an intimate or stately speech. I don't know: perhaps after all it is simply Protestantism that has drained this country artistically.

OUR PILGRIM SEES ANIMALS AND FAMOUS PEOPLE

I would be ashamed if I hadn't been to the Zoo and to Kew Gardens because you should know everything. I even saw elephants bathing and panthers warming their silken bellies in the evening sun. I peeped into the terrifying mouth of a hippopotamus, similar to huge, cows' lungs. I marvelled at the giraffes which smile delicately and reservedly like ageing misses. I saw how a lion sleeps, how monkeys copulate and an orangutan puts a basket on its head as we people do a hat. An Indian peacock spread out its fan for me and turned around, raking challengingly with its claw. The fish in the aquarium flared with all the colours of the rainbow and a rhinoceros seemed to be trapped in a skin which had been sewn for an even larger brute. Well, enough, I have listed enough; I don't want to see anything more.

However, since I wasn't able to draw a stag from memory last time, I ran to Richmond Park where there are whole herds of them. They approach people without ceremony, prefering vegetarians. Although it is quite a hard task to hit a stag, I managed to draw a

whole herd. Behind them a couple of lovers were lingering in the grass. I didn't include them in my picture because what they were doing lovers do in our country too, only not so publicly.

I was covered with sweat in the tropical greenhouses at Kew, among the palm trees, lianas and everything which grows wild on this crazy earth. I went to look at a soldier who runs in front of the Tower in a huge lambskin cap and red coat and who stamps at you at every turn, as strangely as if a dog were raking sand with its hind legs. I don't know what historical event this strange custom refers to. I have also been to Madame Tussaud's.

Madame Tussaud's is a museum of famous people, or at least of their wax figures. The Royal Family are there (also King Alfonso, rather moth-eaten), MacDonald's Cabinet, French presidents, Dickens and Kipling, marshals, Mademoiselle Lenglen, outstanding murderers of the last century and keepsakes of Napoleon such as his socks, belt and hat. In a place of shame there is also Kaiser Wilhelm and Franz Josef, still looking fresh for his age. I stopped next to one particularly effective figure of a gentleman in a top hat and looked in my catalogue to see who it was. Suddenly the gentleman with the top hat moved and left. It was ghastly. After a while two young ladies looked in their catalogue to see whom I represented.

I made a rather unpleasant discovery at Madame Tussaud's: either I am wholly incapable of reading people's faces or else physiognomies are misleading. So, for example, at first sight a seated gentleman with a goatee beard, No. 12, fascinated me. In the catalogue I found, '12: Thomas Neill Cream, executed 1892. Poisoned Matilda Clover with strychnine. He was also found guilty of the murders of three other women.' Truly, his face is very suspicious. Number 13: Franz Müller, murdered Mr. Briggs in a train; hmm. Number 20, a shaven gentleman looking almost honourable: Arthur Devereux, executed 1905, the so-called 'trunk murderer' since he concealed the corpses of his victims in trunks. Horrible. Number 21:—no, this venerable cleric can't be 'Mrs. Deyer, the Reading infant murderess'. I find that I have confused the catalogue's pages and am forced to correct my impressions: the seated gentleman, No. 12, is only Bernard Shaw, No. 13 is Louis Blériot and No. 20 is simply Guglielmo Marconi.

Never again will I judge people by their faces.

CLUBS

How to say it modestly? Well, yes, I received the unde-
served honour, which doesn't happen to every wayfarer,
of being taken to some of the most exclusive clubs in
London. I will try to describe how they look. I have
forgotten the name of the first and I don't even know
which street it was in but they led me through a
medieval passageway, then to the left and right and
then somewhere else, up to a house with completely
blank windows, and then inside. It was like a shed and
from there one went to a cellar and there was the club.
There were boxers there and men of letters and beautiful girls, oak tables and an earthen floor and a room
the size of a postage stamp, a fantastic and awful hole.
I thought that they would kill me there but they gave
me something to eat on earthenware plates and were
kind and nice. Afterwards a South African champion of
running and jumping led me out and to this day I
remember a pretty girl who learnt some Czech from
me.

The second club is famous, ancient and immensely
venerable. Dickens often sat in it and Herbert Spencer

56

and many others, all of whom the resident head waiter or majordomo or porter (or whoever he was) named for me. Perhaps he had also read them all because he seemed to be very refined and stately, as keepers of records usually are. He led me through the whole, historical palace. He showed me the library, the reading room, the old engravings, the heated lavatories, the bathrooms, some historical easy chairs, some halls where gentlemen smoke, other halls where they write and smoke and others where they smoke and read.

Everywhere exhales an air of splendour and old, leather armchairs. My word, if we had such old, leather chairs, we would also have a tradition. Just imagine what historical continuity would be generated if F. Götz could sit in Zákrejs' chair, Šrámek in Šmilovský's and Professor Rádl, let us say, in the late-departed

Hattala's. Our tradition isn't rooted in such old and above all comfortable armchairs. Since it doesn't have anything to sit on, it hangs in the air. I thought about this as I nestled into one of these historical easy chairs. I felt a little historical myself but otherwise quite comfortable and I had a peep at the historical personalities who in part hung on the walls and in part sat in the armchairs reading *Punch* or *Who's Who*. No-one spoke, which has a truly dignified effect. We ought to have such places where people are silent in our country. An elderly gentleman shuffles across the room on two sticks and no-one maliciously tells him that he looks exceptionally well. Another gentleman scours the newspaper (I can't see his face) without

feeling an ardent need to speak to someone about politics. A person from the Continent adds importance to himself by speaking; an Englishman by remaining silent. It seemed to me that all the people who were there were Members of the Royal Academy, the illustrious dead or former Ministers, because none of them spoke. No-one looked at me as I walked in and no-one as I left. I wanted to be like them but I didn't know where to direct my eyes. When I don't speak I look around and when I don't look around I think of strange or humorous things and so I happened to laugh out loud. No-one looked to see what had happened to me; it was crushing. I understood that a sort of ritual was taking place to which belong smoking a pipe, leafing through *Who's Who* and especially remaining silent. This silence isn't the silence of the solitary man or the silence of the Pythagorean philosopher or silence before God or the silence of death or mute meditation; it is a special, social, sophisticated silence, the silence of a gentleman among gentlemen.

I also went to other clubs. There are many hundreds of them of differing character and purpose but the best are all in Piccadilly or its environs and have old, leather armchairs, a ritual of silence, impeccable waiters and a restriction on women. As you see, these are great advantages. Apart from this, they are built in classical style, from stone which is black with smoke and white with rain. Inside there is good cuisine, huge halls, silence, tradition, hot and cold water, some portraits and billiard tables and a lot of other memorable things. There are also political clubs and women's clubs and night clubs but I didn't go to those.

At this point, some reflections would be appropriate on social life, male monasticism, good cooking, old portraits, the English character and other, related issues, but as a wayfaring man I have to go on to more and more, new discoveries.

THE BIGGEST SAMPLES FAIR
OR THE BRITISH EMPIRE EXHIBITION

I

If I were to tell you in advance what there is most of at the exhibition at Wembley, then it is definitely people; and schools outings. It is true that I am a friend of populousness, reproduction, children, schools and practical education but I confess that at moments I wished I had had a machine gun so that I could have cleared a path through the runaway, jostling, scurrying, stamping herd of boys with round caps on their bonces or chains of girls holding hands so that they wouldn't get lost. In time and with endless patience I managed to reach a stand. They were selling New Zealand apples there, or rice blooms were on display from Australia, or a billiard table produced in the Bahamas. I even had the good fortune to cast eyes on a statue of the Prince of Wales made of Canadian butter, which filled me with regret that most of London's monuments aren't also made of butter. After which, I was again shunted on by the stream of people and given up to the view of a fat gentleman's throat or

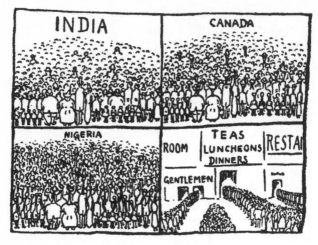

the ear of the old lady in front of me. Otherwise, I didn't object at all. How people would jostle if in the Australian cold storage section fat gentlemen's ruddy throats were on display or baskets of old ladies' dried ears in the Nigerian clay palace.

Helpless, I relinquish my intention of presenting an illustrated guide to the Wembley exhibition. How should I describe this horn of commercial plenty? There are stuffed sheep here, dried plums, armchairs produced in Fiji, mountains of dammar or tin ore, festoons of mutton legs, dried copra like huge bunions, pyramids of cans, rubber lampshades, old English furniture from South African factories, Syrian raisins, sugarcane, walking sticks and cheese; and New Zealand brushes, sweets from Hong Kong, some Malaysian oils, Australian perfumes, a model of some tin mines, gramophones from Jamaica and mountain ranges of butter from Canada. As you see, it is a journey around the world, or rather a wander through an excessively large bazaar. Never in my life have I been in such a gigantic hubbub.

The palace of engineering is beautiful; and the most beautiful works of British, plastic art are locomotives, ships, boilers, turbines, transformers, some strange machines with two horns on their foreheads, machines for all sorts of rotating, shaking and banging, monstrous beasts which are far more fantastical and infinitely more elegant than the saurians in the Natural History Museum. I don't know what they are called or what one does with them but they are beautiful; and sometimes a mere screw nut (a hundred pounds in weight) is the height of formal perfection. Some machines are red like paprika, others massive and grey, some striped with brass and others black and magnificent like a tomb. And it is strange that an age which has invented two columns and seven steps in front of every house has produced in metal such poetic, inexhaustible peculiarity of form and function. And now just imagine that this is huddled together in an area larger than Wenceslas Square, that it is larger than the Uffizi and Vatican collections put together, that it mostly rotates, hisses, grinds with oiled valves, clicks with steel jaws, sweats greasily and shines with brass. It is the myth of the metal age. The only perfection which modern civilisation achieves is mechanical; machines are magnificent and immaculate but the life which serves them or is served by them isn't magnificent or shiny or more perfect or more comely. Even the work of machines isn't perfect. Only They, the machines themselves, are like gods. And so that you know, I found a true idol in the Palace of Industry. It is a revolving, impregnable safe, a lustrous, armour-plated ball which quietly revolves and revolves on a black altar. It is strange and a little grisly.

Bear me homewards, *Flying Scotsman*, splendid, one-hundred-and-fifty-ton locomotive. Bear me across the sea, white and shining ship. There I will sit in the wasteground among wild thyme and close my eyes, for I have rustic blood and what I have seen has disquieted me a little. This perfection of matter from which the perfection of man doesn't accrue, these radiant machines from a difficult and unredeemed life, disturb me. Oh, *Flying Scotsman*, what would the blind beggar who sold me matches today look like next to you? He was blind and consumed by scurvy; he was a very poor and faulty machine; he was just a man.

II

Besides machines, the exhibition at Wembley presents two spectacles: raw materials and products. The raw materials are usually more beautiful and more interesting. There is something more perfect about a block of pure tin than an engraved and beaten, tin bowl. Red or fiery-grey timber from somewhere in Guyana or Sarawak is decidedly more attractive than a finished billiard table, and slimily translucent, crude rubber from Ceylon or Malaysia is actually far more beautiful and mysterious than rubber carpeting or a rubber steak. And I won't even describe the various African grains, nuts from God knows where, berries, seeds, pips, fruits, stones, galingales, ears, poppy heads, tubers, legumes, piths and fibres and roots and leaves, things which are dried, powdery, oily and scaly, in all manner of colours and tangible qualities, whose names, mostly very beautiful, I have forgotten and whose use rather intrigues me. I believe that ultimately these are used to grease machines, imitate flour and butter suspicious-looking tarts in mass-feeding establishments in Lyons. Of course, these incandescent, striped, deep purple, tawny and metallic-sounding woods are used to make old English furniture and not

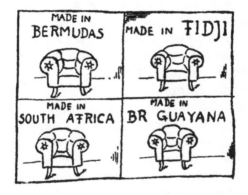

negro idols or temples or thrones for black or brown kings. At the most, only bast baskets or sacks in which the wealth of the British Empire's trade goods was gathered here tell anything of the negro or Malaysian hand which left its imprint on them in its strange and pretty, technical handwriting. Everything else is a European product. But I mustn't lie: not everything else. There are several recognised exotic industries which Europeans delight in, as for example the Indian mass production of Buddhas, Chinese fans, Cashmere scarves or damascene swords. And so seated Śākyamunis are produced in large quantities, aniline lacquers, Chinese porcelain for export, elephants made of ivory and inkwells made of viper's bugloss or talc, engraved bowls, mother-of-pearl follies and other, exotic products, guaranteed genuine. There is no folk art anymore; the black man in Benin carves figures from elephants' tusks as if he had studied at the Münich Academy and if you were to give him a piece of wood he would carve an armchair out of it. Well, good God, obviously he has ceased being a savage and has become—what, actually?—yes, he has become an employee of civilised industry.

There are four hundred million coloured people in the British Empire and at the British Empire Exhibition the only trace of them is in a few advertising dummies, a couple of yellow or brown stallkeepers and several old relics which somehow found their way here for reasons of curiosity and amusement. And I don't know whether it is a terrible bankruptcy of the coloured races or a terrible silence of four hundred million people; nor do I know which of these two would be the more horrible.

The British Empire Exhibition is huge and full-to-bursting. There is everything here, even a stuffed lion and the extinct emu. Only the spirit of four hundred million coloured people is missing. It is an exhibition of English trade. It is a cross-section of that feeble tier of European interests which has covered the whole world, none too mindful of what is underneath. The Exhibition at Wembley shows what four hundred million people do for Europe and partly also what Europe does for them. But there is nothing here of what they do for themselves. There isn't much of this in the British Museum either. The largest colonial empire doesn't have a true ethnographic museum…

But be gone from me, evil thoughts. Let me rather be shunted and pushed by a stream of people, from New Zealand apples to Guinea coconuts, from Singapore tin to South African gold ore. Let me see distances and geographical zones, the minerals and fruits of the earth, mementos of animals and people, everything from which, ultimately, rustling pound notes are pressed. Everything is here which it is possible to turn into money and to buy and sell, from a handful of grain to a Pullman carriage, from a piece of coal to a blue fox fur. My soul, what would you like to buy from these treasures of the world? Nothing, nothing, actually. I would like to be very small and to stand again in old Prouza's shop in Úpice, to have my eyes boggle at the black gingerbread, pepper, ginger, vanilla and bay leaves and to think that they are all the treasures of the earth and all the scents of Arabia and all the spices of distant lands, to be astonished, sniff and then run off and read a Jules Verne novel about strange, distant and uncommon parts.

For I, foolish soul, imagined them differently.

THE EAST END

It begins not far from the centre of the world, the Bank of England, the Stock Exchange and a jungle of other banks and exchange offices. This Gold Coast is almost lapped by the black waves of the east of London. 'Don't go there without a guide,' the Westenders told me, 'and don't take much money with you.' Well, that is decidedly an exaggeration. To my mind, Piccadilly or Fleet Street are a worse wilderness than the Isle of Dogs or the infamous Limehouse, even with its Chinatown, or than Poplar lock, stock and barrel, with its Jews, sailors and wretched Rotherhithe on the other side of the river. Nothing happened to me; I only came back very sad, although I have weathered sorties into Košíře and the harbour abominations of Marseilles and Palermo. It is true that there are hideous streets made of filthy bricks, with hordes of children in the street, with strange, Chinese types who scurry like shadows under even stranger shops, with drunken sailors, charitable shelters, blood-stained youths and a stench of singed rags; but I have seen worse places, screaming destitution, as dirty and inflamed as an ulcer,

inexpressible stenches and dens worse than a wolf's lair. But that is not it, that is not it. What is terrible in East London isn't what one can see and smell but that there is so enormously and irredeemably much of it. Elsewhere poverty and ugliness are like a rubbish heap between two houses, like a hideous nook, fistula or unclean drain; but here there are miles and miles of black houses, hopeless streets, Jewish stores, superfluous children, gin palaces and Christian shelters. Miles and miles, from Peckham to Hackney, from Walworth to Barking: Bermondsey, Rotherhithe, Poplar, Bromley, Stepney Bow and Bethnal Green, quarters of labourers, Jews, Cockneys and stevedores from the docks, people who are poor and hopeless— everything equally nondescript, black, bare and endless, cut through by dirty channels of noisy thoroughfares and always equally dismal. And in the south, in the north-west, in the north-east, again the same: miles and miles of black houses where the whole street is only an enormous, horizontal tenement, factories, gasometers, railway tracks, clayey commons, storehouses for commodities and storehouses for people, without end and without hope. There are certainly more hideous quarters and more destitute streets in all parts of the world; even destitution has a higher standard here and the poorest beggar still isn't bound in rags. But, my God, what people, what sorts of millions of people live in this larger half of London, in these short, uniform, joyless streets which swarm on the map of London like worms in immense carrion.

And that is exactly the misery of the East End: there is too much of it; and it is impossible to transform it. Not even a demon tempter would dare to say, 'If you want, I'll destroy this city and rebuild it in three days, new and better, not so black, not so mechanical, not so inhuman and desolate.' If he said this perhaps I would fall down and worship him. I have wandered through streets whose names evoke Jamaica, Canton, India or Peking. All are the same; in all the windows there are little, lace curtains. They might almost seem decent if there weren't five hundred thousand of these barracks. In this overwhelming quantity it no longer looks like housing for people but like a geological formation; this black magma is disgorged by factories or is the dregs of the trade which sails up the Thames in white ships or has built up in layers of soot and dust. Go and take a look at Oxford Street and Regent

Street and the Strand, at what beautiful houses people have built for goods, for products and for things because man's products have their value. A shirt would lose in value if it had to be sold within such grey, sterile walls; but a person can live here, that is, sleep, eat revolting food and breed children.

Perhaps someone more knowledgeable would take you to more picturesque places where even filth is romantic and destitution quaint, but I have strayed into streets of great number and I can't find my way out. Or is it at all certain where these numberless, black streets lead?

THE COUNTRY

Well then, take a seat on a train and travel off in any direction, singing to yourself to the rattle of the wheels, 'which way out, which way out'. And the Streets of Great Number will fly past, the drums of the gasometers, the railway crossings, the factories and cemeteries. Now strips of green break into the endless city; you see the last tram stop, quiet suburbs, green grass and the first little sheep bowed towards the earth in Nature's eternal ritual of eating. Then another half

an hour and you are out of the largest city in the world. You get out at a small station where hospitable people are waiting for you and you are in the English countryside.

Where are you going to come by pretty words now to describe the quiet and green charms of the English countryside? I have been down in Surrey and up in Essex; I have rambled along roads serrated with hedges, the same hedges which make England truly England because they demarcate without confining. Half-open gates lead you to ancient lanes in a park deeper than a forest and here there is a little, red house with high chimneys, a church steeple among the trees, a meadow with herds of cows, herds of horses which turn their beautiful, serious eyes on you, a pathway which looks as if it has been swept, velvet pools with water lilies and irises, parks, country houses, meadows and meadows, not a single field, nothing which might cry of human toil, a paradise where God Himself has laid paths of asphalt and sand, planted old trees and braided covers out of ivy for the red houses. My uncle, Czech peasant farmer, how you would shake your head with indignation looking at the red and black herds of cows on the most beautiful meadows in the world and say, 'What a waste of such beautiful dung!' And you would say, 'Why don't they sow turnips here? And here, people, here there could be wheat and here potatoes and here in place of this shrubbery I would plant cherry trees and sour cherry trees and here lucerne and here oats and here on this land rye or rapeseed. Why, there's earth here, people, that's fit for spreading on bread and they leave it to pasture!' You know, uncle, apparently it isn't worth the work here. For the information, wheat comes here from

Australia and sugar from India and potatoes from
Africa or somewhere. You know, uncle, there aren't any
peasants here anymore and this is only a sort of a
garden. 'And you know, my boy,' you would say, 'I like
it more the way it is in our country. Perhaps it's only a
turnip but at least you can see the work. And here,
well, here no-one even looks after these cows and
sheep. It's a wonder that no-one steals them! Good
heavens, my boy, why, there isn't a person in sight;
only someone over there riding a bicycle and here,
damn it, someone in one of those stinking cars again.
My boy, my boy, does no-one graft around here?'

I would have difficulty in explaining the economic
system of England to my uncle; his palms would itch
too much for the heavy ploughshare. The English
countryside isn't for working in; it is for looking at. It
is as green as a park and as untouched as paradise. I
strolled along a grassy path in Surrey in moist rain,

among tufts of yellowy blossoming broom and red heather sprouting through light bracken; and there was nothing there but the sky and rounded hillocks because the houses and their people are hidden in a cluster of trees from whence a delightful cloudlet emits the scents of a prepared lunch. I am thinking of you, good, old house with your raftered ceiling and huge hearth by which a whole, sodden person can snuggle himself comfortably. The table is oaken and very pala-table is the Guildford beer in clay tankards and the speech of merry people over English bacon and cheese. Once more, thank you and now I must go on.

I roamed like a fairy over grassy plots in Essex, climbed over a hedge into a seignorial park and saw water lilies and gladstonia in a black pool, I danced a dance in a granary which I didn't know, climbed up a church steeple and twenty times a day marvelled at the harmony and perfection of the life with which the Englishman surrounds himself at home. The English

home is tennis and warm water, a gong summoning you to lunch, books, meadows, comfort which is selected, fixed and blessed by the centuries, free children and the patriarchalism of parents and a hospitality and formality as comfortable as a dressing gown. In short, the English home is the English home and so I have drawn it as a memento, even with its cuckoo and rabbit. Inside, one of the most reasonable men in the world lives and writes and outside a cuckoo cuckoos perhaps thirty times in succession. Thus I end my tale of the best things in England.

CAMBRIDGE AND OXFORD

At first one has the impression of a provincial town; and suddenly, good gracious, whose is this old castle? It is a students' residence with three courtyards, its own chapel, a regal hall where the students eat, a park, playing fields and I don't know what else. And

here is another, even larger, with four courtyards, a park beyond the river, its own cathedral, a still larger, Gothic refectory, five-hundred-year-old beams, a gallery of old portraits, even older traditions and yet more famous names. The third is the oldest, the fourth is distinguished for scholarship, the fifth for athletics records, the sixth for the prettiest chapel, the seventh for I know not what; and because there are at least fifteen of them I have confused them all. I see only castle-like palaces in Perpendicular Style and huge courtyards where gentlemen pupils amble in black gowns and four-sided caps with a tassel, each of whom has two or three rooms to himself in the wings of these castles. I see Gothic chapels gutted by Protestantism, banquetting halls with a dais for the 'masters' and 'fellows' and venerable, smoked portraits of earls, statesmen and poets who went down from here. I see the celebrated 'backs', that is to say, the rear sides of the colleges above the river Cam, over which bridges are pitched to ancient college parks. I float on the gentle river between the backs and the parks and think of our students, of their scrawny bellies and shoes worn out by tramping to lectures. I bow down to you, Cambridge, because I received the honour of eating on a dais among learned 'masters' in a hall as vast and old, it seemed to me, as if I had only dreamt it. Hail to you with both arms, Cambridge, because I received the pleasure of eating from earthenware dishes at the Half-Moon with students, masters and other young people; and I was happy among them.

And I saw lawns on which only a 'master' may tread and never an 'undergraduate', and stairs on which only a 'graduate' may play marbles and never a 'student'. I saw professors in rabbits' fur and robes as red as a lobster. I saw graduates kneel and kiss the hand of the Vice-Chancellor. Of all these wonders I was able only to draw a venerable college provost who poured me a glass of sherry at least as old as Pitt the Elder.

From memory I then drew some Cambridge colleges as they had appeared to me several times in dreams. In reality they are even larger and more beautiful.

Sometimes I also dream about the Cambridge rabbit. They gave him some gas to breathe to see what his rabbity spleen would say to it. I saw him die; he breathed frantically and his eyes bulged. Now he haunts me in my dreams. God be gracious to his long-eared soul.

What evil should I now speak of Oxford? I can't praise Oxford, having praised Cambridge; and my friendship with Cambridge compels me to rain fire and brimstone on conceited Oxford. Unfortunately, I rather

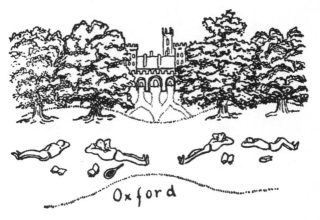

liked it there. The colleges are even larger and perhaps even older. They have beautiful, quiet parks, galleries of equally famous forebears, banquetting halls, monuments and dignified porters. But all this pomp and tradition isn't for everyone. It seems that its object isn't to raise erudite specialists but gentlemen. Imagine our students lunching at the least in the Wallenstein hall, on weighty, old silver, served by waiters in livery and prepared for examinations by private tutors in lecture halls equipped with all manner of armchairs, rocking chairs and easy chairs. Imagine—but no; boys, don't bother about it.

OUR PILGRIM VISITS SOME CATHEDRALS

Cathedral cities are small towns with large cathedrals in which enormously long services are held and a verger comes and instructs the tourist not to look at the ceiling and the pillars but to sit down in a pew and listen to what is being sung from the chancel. The vergers have this custom in Ely, Lincoln, York and Durham. I don't know what they do elsewhere because I haven't been elsewhere. I have heard a vast number of litanies, psalms, anthems and hymns and I have noticed that English cathedrals usually have wooden ceilings, as a result of which the buttress system of Continental Gothic hasn't been developed in them; that Perpendicular pillars in England have the appearance of complicated pipes; that Protestant vergers are more severe than their Catholic counterparts and stand just as much on tips as Italian vergers, except that, being gentlemen, they have to receive more; and that the Reformation carried out some very swinish business when it struck off the heads of statues and removed pictures and other pagan idolatries from the churches. As a result,

English cathedrals are bare and odd, as if no-one had moved into them. And even worse is that in the centre of the main nave there is an enclosed chancel for the priest, ministrants and elite of the parish; the rest of the people sit below and see nothing more than the more or less carved walls of the chancel and the rear of the organ. The main nave is thoroughly impaired by this and the whole area is cut in two. In all my life I have never seen anything so absurd. But because they are still singing something in the chancel, I must gather my things and go.

Ely, Ely, la'ma sabach-tha'ni! You betrayed me, Ely, dead town lying at the foot of a Romanesque cathedral, when, tired and thirsty at five o'clock in the afternoon, I beat on the doors of tea-rooms and pubs, bars, newsagents' and stationers' but wasn't admitted. At five o'clock in the afternoon Ely sleeps. Unfortunately I haven't had time to ascertain what Ely does at three o'clock in the afternoon or at ten o'clock in the morning; perhaps she only ever sleeps. I also sat among cowpats in a public park and observed the venerable cathedral which stands there to the praise of God. Those jackdaws around the towers are perhaps the souls of vergers who haunted people in the church while they were alive.

Lincoln runs up to a little hill, has a small castle, a cathedral and something left by the Romans but I forget what. The cathedral is hoary and beautiful and they sing services there for three vergers who are eyeing me maliciously. What can I do? Farewell, vergers, I am going to take a look at York.

In York the cathedral is even more beautiful. I want to have a look around but the verger tells me that I should leave off, like, that there's going to be a service in a while. I also went to stroll along the city walls and

drew York Minster from there although a service was taking place; perhaps for this reason I shall go to the English hell. Round about is pretty Yorkshire, a landscape of heavy cows and celebrated pigs, centre of all English hams and bacon. And the streets in York are old and pretty, with protruding gables and black rafters. I could say a lot about the history of York but I have to go to Durham.

The cathedral in Durham is ancient and looms on a high rock. Inside, services are held with preaching, singing and vergers. Nevertheless, I saw the grave of the Venerable Bede, hefty pillars and cloisters and an outing of pretty American girls. These pillars are heavily covered with condensed fluting which gives a strange, almost polychromatic impression. Apart from this, there is the grave of St. Cuthbert, an old castle and old, stone houses, and the pretty, little town runs from hill to hill, and more than this I do not know.

So, English cathedral architecture on the whole is less painted and less plastic than Continental architecture. When the pre-Norman Britons had once succeeded in building enormous cathedral naves with wooden ceilings they persevered in this even into the Gothic period, obviously out of primeval conservatism. And their churches are vast halls with wide windows, without vaulted and ribbed ceilings, without a powerfully prominent system of buttresses, vaults, pinnacles and all that plastic frenzy. They also have two tetragonal towers over the portal and one above the transept, statues swept out by the Reformation and poor sculptural decoration, inner space spoiled by the chancel and the organ and an overall impression strongly upset by the presence of vergers.

However, one more word about you, little churches without choirs and vergers, bare and cool halls of God with oak ceilings, grassy cemeteries around them and

a tetragonal tower among the trees which is as typical of the English countryside as onion-shaped cupolas are of our countryside, towers which chime off the hours in an eternally unvaried, ecclesiastical strain over the eternally unvaried graves of the deceased.

JOURNEY TO SCOTLAND

EDINBURGH

And now to the north, to the north! County after county drifts by. In some, cows are lying down, in some they are standing, in some places sheep are grazing, elsewhere horses and elsewhere only crows. A grey sea appears, rocks and marshes. The hedges cease and in their place stretch low, stone walls. Stone walls, stone hamlets and stone towns; beyond the river Tweed it is a stone country.

Mr. Bone was almost right when he pronounced Edinburgh the prettiest city in the world. It is pretty, stone-grey and odd. Where in other places a river flows, here a railway runs; on one side there is the old town, on the other side the new; there are roads which are as wide as nowhere else, a statue or a church in every vista and horribly tall houses in the old town which don't exist anywhere in England; and washing, fluttering on lines above the streets like flags of all the nations: that too does not exist down in England; and grimy, red-headed children in the streets: that too does not exist down in England; and blacksmiths, joiners and all sorts of gaffers: that too does not exist in

England; and strange, little streets, 'wynds' or 'closes': that too does not exist in England; and fat, dishevelled, old women: that too does not exist in England: here the people begin again as in Naples or as in our country. It seems strange: here, these old houses have chimneys at the front as if in place of towers, as I have drawn. This exists nowhere else in the world than in Edinburgh. And the city lies on little hills. You are rushing somewhere and suddenly you find a green chasm under your feet with a pretty river below; you are walking and out of nowhere another street runs across a bridge above your head, as in Genoa; you are walking and you come upon a neatly circular square, as in Paris. Always you have something to astonish you. You reach the Parliament building and whole flocks of lawyers are running about in periwigs with two tails at the back, just as

89

some hundred years ago. You scurry to look at the castle which stands so picturesquely on a vertical rock and a whole band of pipers and a company of Highlanders step into your path. These have checked, plaid trousers and a cap with ribbons, but the pipers have short, red and black kilts and on them little pouches made of leather and they play a bleating and stirring song on their bagpipes to the accompaniment of a whole band of drummers. Drumsticks fly above the drummers' heads, they circle, hop about in a strange and savage dance and the pipers bleat a war song and march along the castle esplanade with their bare knees and diminutive, ballerina's steps. And boom, boom, the drumsticks spin faster, they inter-cross, soar up and suddenly it becomes a funeral march, the pipers squeak an endless and drawn-out melody, the Highlanders stand to attention with the castle of the Scottish kings behind them and even further behind them the whole, bloody and terrible history of this country. And boom, boom, the drum-sticks dance a wild and skilful dance overhead: here music has remained a spectacle, as it was in primeval times, and the pipers inflate themselves as if, with a stallion's impatience, they were dancing into battle.

A different country and different people. It is a province, but it is monumental; it is a poorer country, but brisk; a russet and angular type of people, but the girls are prettier than down in England; beautiful, runny-nosed children and a square-shouldered, manly life despite all Calvinism. Upon my soul, I took quite a liking to it here. And I am pleased to give you, as a little extra, a strip of the sea near Leith and Newhaven, a cold and steely sea and blue shellfish as a keepsake and a greeting from the fishing boats. And I will also add the ancient and picturesque little town of Stirling with its castle of the Scottish kings. If you stand near the old cannon on the castle promontory you have the key to the Scottish mountains in your hand. What if we went and had a look there?

A ballerina trips in front of the castle with a bayonet and a chequered kilt. Ten steps to the gate, ten back, attention, present arms, order arms. The ballerina shakes out her short skirt and dances back. To the south the battleground of Robert Bruce, to the north blue mountains and down in the green meadow the river Forth meanders in a way that no other river in the world meanders; and I have drawn it so that everyone can see that it is a beautiful and satisfying river.

RIVER FORTH

LOCH TAY

If I were a poet like Karel Toman or Otokar Fischer I would write you a poem today which wasn't long but beautiful. It would be about the Scottish lochs; it would be blown through by the Scottish wind and bedewed by the daily, Scottish rain. There would be something there about the blue waves, the heaths, the bracken and the melancholy paths. I wouldn't include the fact that these melancholy paths are generally fenced in (perhaps so that witches can't go and dance there). I must say in crude prose how beautiful it is here: a blue and purple lake between bare hills (this lake bears the name of Loch Tay and every valley is called Glen, every mountain Ben and every person Mac), a blue and peaceful lake, a wind blowing sparks, black or red-haired bullocks in the meadows, pitch-black torrents and tragically deserted hills and over-grown grass and heaths. How should I describe it to you? It would be best after all to write in verse but nothing comes to mind to rhyme with 'wind'.

Yesterday evening the very same wind blew me to Finlarig Castle. I scared the old castle attendant half to death because at that very moment he was cleaning the former place of execution and perhaps mistook me for a ghost. When he had calmed down he held forth in a strange dialect but with great passion about the aforementioned place of execution. There is a hole there through which the severed heads fell into a place beneath the ground. As for me, I consider it possible that this aperture and the underground chamber, very similar to a cesspit, served a bloodless and quite natural function. An American who was present grinned at all of it sceptically as if it were humbug, but Americans lack a fair perspective on the secrets of the Old World. Old grandpa attendant was unusually proud of his castle. He pointed out all manner of trees, old horseshoes and stones and held forth for an immensely long time, obviously in Gaelic, about Queen Mary Stuart, Marquis Ballochbuich and Scottish history. There is also a chamber there with statues in it. One represents Queen Mary, another a knight called Campbell and another a Queen's jester. This is the one I have drawn for you.

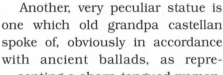

Another, very peculiar statue is one which old grandpa castellan spoke of, obviously in accordance with ancient ballads, as representing a sharp-tongued woman; and because this couldn't go on any longer, the sheriff decided that all those who were afflicted should publicly slap her backside, which the statue in question apparently depicts. At this point I differ with the local authority in that this statue seems far older than the sheriff, the mouthy woman or Finlarig Castle; I think it represents something ancient, perhaps the suffering of the damned in hell. Incidentally, I have drawn it very carefully.

I also succeeded in drawing a couple of Scots, a man and his wife. Scots are mostly thickset, florid people with strong necks. They have a lot of children and the congenial, ancient names of clans. They only wear skirts or 'kilts' if they are in the army or if they are playing the bagpipes. Their checked plaids are called 'tartans' and are actually types of coats of arms. Each clan has a differently coloured tartan, which of course was once sufficient reason for

mutual slaughter with a differently chequered clan.

The Scottish Sunday is even worse than the English one and Scottish church services evoke the notion of infinity. The pastors wear bristly whiskers and they aren't as rosy and benign as English clergymen. Throughout the whole of Scotland trains stop travelling on Sunday, the stations close and absolutely nothing happens; I am surprised that even the clocks don't stop. Only the wind ruffles the pallid, steely lakes between the bare domes of the hills. I went out sailing on one of those lakes, until my boat ran aground on a sandbank. I also put my pen down and went wandering along the melancholy paths between the wire fences.

*

And another Scotland appeared to me beneath the grey skies: long, desolate glens with ruined, stone shanties; low, stone walls running along the hillsides; for miles and miles hardly a stone house that doesn't seem unoccupied; here and there fields of oats with a crop a finger high; everything else only bracken and stones and grass as stiff as moss. In some places sheep bleat without a shepherd, creeping along a hillside; sometimes a bird shrieks plaintively; down below, the black-cum-yellow foaming river Dochart roars among knotty oak trees. A strange, hard, almost prehistoric country. Clouds drag over the tops of the hills, a veil of rain eclipses the gloomy, empty region which hasn't yet been subdued by the hand of man; and down below, the black river Dochart roars over black stones.

'BINNORIE, O BINNORIE'

Bear me, *Mistress of the Lake*, across the keenly grey and blue Loch Tay, between the unfrequented domes of the hills, beneath the heavens which regale me with rain and shine. Bear me, tidy boat, across the shimmering silk of Loch Tay.

Bear me, red postal service, through the greenest of green valleys, the valley of knotty trees, the valley of the foaming river, the valley of shaggy sheep and the glen of Nordic plenty. Wait, silver aspen; stay, outstretched,

curly oak, black pinewood and solid alder; wait, young woman with the wild eyes.

But no, carry me, hissing train, to the north, to the north, through these black mountains. Blue and black mountains above green mounds, a valley of red-haired cows, light and dark greenery, glossy lakes and the Nordic beauty of the birches, endless, bare and graceful, rounded hills with dales and dells, overgrown glens and hillsides russet with heather, the northern beauty of the meadows, birch thickets and in the north, in the north, the surface of the sea glints like a steel blade.

Inverness: a little town of trout and Highlanders, completely built out of pink granite. And these timber houses are made of such nicely-hewn ashlar that I have drawn them for you. And these little roofs above the doors are found only in Inverness.

And now to the mountains, to the heart of the country, to the region of the Gaelic tongue. My God, I have never seen such a sad and terrible region: again these bare hills but higher and more horrible; nothing but dwarf birches and then not even those but oozing, black peat and on it only flakes of bog cotton which we call St. Ivan's Beard and then not even that but stones, nothing but stones and rigid clusters of rushes.

The clouds drag across the grey, bald patches of the hills and spout rain, hazes rise above the black rocks and a sombre glen appears, as sad as the howling of a dog. For miles and miles there is neither a house nor a human; and when a house does fly past it is grey and stone like these rocks and is isolated, isolated for miles around. A lake without a fisherman, streams without a miller, sheep country without a shepherd, ways without a wayfarer. Only in the most ample dell do shaggy, Scottish bulls graze, stand in the rain and lie down in the marshes; perhaps that is why they are so overgrown with shaggy locks of hair, as I have drawn them for you.

And Scottish sheep have complete invernesses made of wool and seem to have black masks on their faces. No-one tends them; only low, stone walls extend along the desolate hillsides marking the presence of man: 'Up to this wall it is my pasture'.

And now it is so desolate here that there are no longer either herds or property, only a ruined house and a decayed mound on the brown of an oozing, moss-grown hillside. The end of life. Here perhaps nothing has changed for ten thousand years; people have only brought roads here and built railway lines, but the earth hasn't changed. Nowhere are there either trees or thickets, only a cold lake, horsetail and bracken, brown heaths without end, black stones without end, inky, shadowy, mountain peaks cut through by the silver threads of torrents, black muds in the peat bogs, cloudily smoking glens between the bare ridges of the mountain-tops, and another lake with sombre rushes, its surface empty of birds, a region empty of people, anxiety without a cause, a road without a goal. I don't know what I'm looking for, but this finally is solitude. Drink of this enormous sadness before you return among people, swell with solitude, unsatiated soul, for you have never seen anything greater than this desolation.

And now they are taking me to the valley. On the ridges, yellow sparks of broom shoot forth, dwarf pine crouches, stunted birch trees have clutched at granite rubble, a black torrent bounds through the valley, the pine forests are already here, the rhododendron and red foxglove blossom purple, birch trees, Arolla pines, oaks and alders, a Nordic wilderness, bracken up to your waist and a virgin juniper forest; the sun breaks through the clouds and, below, a deep groove of new sea glints between the mountain peaks.

TERRA HYPERBOREA

I am in a region which is called Skye, that is to say
'Sky', although I am not in the heavens but only in the
Hebrides, on a large, strange island among other
islands, on an island consisting of fjords, peat, rocks
and summits. I collect coloured shells among the blue
or flaxen pebbles and by a special grace of heaven even
find the droppings of a wild elk, which is the milch cow
of Gaelic water nymphs. The hillsides drip like a satu-
rated sponge, the bruach heather catches at my feet,
but then, folks, the islands of Raasay and Scalpay,
Rhum and Eigg are visible and then one can see
mountains with strange and ancient names like Beinn
na Callaich and Sgurr na Banachdich and Leacan
Nighean an t-Siosalaich or even Druim nan Cleochd,
whereas these bare domes are called only Blaven, quite
simply Blaven. And this rivulet is simply Aan Reidhe
Mhoire and that sandy, little bay over there is simply
Srón Ard a' Mhullaich. These and all other names
show the beauty and peculiarity of the Isle of Skye.

It is beautiful and poor, and the original shanties
look as prehistoric as if they had been built by the

long-departed Picts, of whom, as is well known, nothing is known. Then the Caledonian Gaels came here and Vikings from somewhere in Norway. King Haakon even left a stone castle behind him and so this place is called Kyleakin. Otherwise these conquerors all left the Isle of Skye in its original state, just as it passed from the hand of God: wild, desolate and furrowed, wet and sublime, terrible and lovely. Little, stone cottages become overgrown with grass and moss or fall into disrepair, abandoned by the people.

Once a week the sun shines and then the mountain peaks are revealed in all their inexpressible shades of blue. There are bluenesses which are azure, pearl, misty or indigo, black, pink and green, bluenesses which are deep, tinged, similar to steam, to a haze or to a mere memory of something beautifully blue. I saw all of these and countless other blues on the blue peaks of the Cuillin, but to top it all there was also a blue sky and a blue bay and this can't be described at all. I tell you, unknown and heavenly virtues arose in me at the sight of this immense blueness.

Loch Coru_h and Cuillim Hills

But then the clouds spring up from the lowlands and the mountains, the sea turns grey and a dank rain merges with the dripping slopes. In the home of some good people peat burns on a hearth, a lady with a Greek profile sings Scottish ballads and I sing a strange and old song with the others:

> Tha tigh'nn fodham, fodham, fodh'm;
> Tha tigh'nn fodham, fodham, fodh'm;
> Tha tigh'nn fodham, fodham, fodh'm;
> Tha tigh'nn fodham éirigh.

Then we all hold hands in a circle and sing something Scottish about parting or meeting again. Between the capes of the islands a narrow strip of open sea can be seen; whales apparently swim this way to Iceland or Greenland. Man, why are you sad when you look at this narrow strip of open sea? Hail to you, lands which I may never see again!

Ah, I have seen blue and fiery seas and silken beaches and palm trees bent over azure waves, but these grey and cool lochs have bewitched me. Look, over there a crane is wading through some seaweed and a gull or sea-swallow is gliding over the waves with a sharp and wild shriek; a snipe is whistling and a flock of fieldfares are whizzing over the heath; a shaggy bullock is surprised by man and sheep graze on the bare hills, similar from a distance to yellow lice. And with the evening, myriads of minute midges swarm out and creep into a person's nose, while the Northern day lasts almost until midnight.

And the pallid, plashing sea beneath one's feet and the open route to the north...

'BUT I AM ANNIE
OF LOCHROYAN'

However, the captain of the little steamer couldn't be coaxed into taking the open route to the north. He was a prudent man and instead of going to Greenland or Iceland he simply sailed to Mallaig; obviously he hadn't read Jack London.

Why are you chasing us, sea gulls, screaming, marine rabble? If I could fly like you I would fly over Scotland, resting on the rounded, little waves of the lochs, and then over the sea to Hamburg. The river Elbe is there and I would fly over it with strong wings. Only at the town of Mělník would I set out along another river until I reached Prague; and I would fly through the triumphal arches of all the bridges, screaming and guffawing with delight: 'People,

I am flying straight from Scotland to warm my white belly in the warm Vltava. Strange and beautiful is that

country, also called Caledonia or the land of Stevenson; but it is somewhat sad and dreary. Here, it is true, there are no lochs, but in place of them we have Wenceslas Square; and here there is no Ladhar Bheinn, but we have embankments with acacias and Vyšehrad and Petřín hill; and I have been asked to pass on the greetings of a pilgrim who is sailing at this moment through the Sound of Sleat.'

I have drawn this Sound of Sleat for you, complete with Ladhar Bheinn. I have also drawn Mallaig

harbour for you and have even added a sailor so that no-one can say that I have perhaps withheld something or that I haven't drawn

107

the world as it is, with its boats and sailors.

Bear me, train, through all the regions of Caledonia, for it is fine here and it makes me feel wistful. And there is Loch Morar and Loch Shiel and there are mountain peaks, ravines and glens, broad-shouldered hills with titanic inclines, vaulted ridges and the rumps of immense, stone, primordial animals with boldly green copses in their armpits and the folds of

Loch Eilt.

their bare bodies, hills planted with rocks like a Dundee cake with almonds, sharp lakes with tender islets such as Loch Eilt and lakes everywhere where the opportunity allows, long and shimmering waters, their surfaces ruffled by the wind, with silver paths for water spirits,

Loch Eil

mountains which are rocky or have risen rounded from a granite dough, hills which are striped, furrowed, as

108

bare as a hippopotamus, blue and red and green, and always the desolate mountains, without end and without people.

At last, Fort William, one of the iron barriers once holding rebellious highlanders; and above it, Ben Nevis, the highest peak in this country of mountains,

ben Nevis

a hefty and cloud-capped fellow above an oceanic fjord interwoven with white waterfalls from the fields of snow up there on the summit,—and still more mountains and mountains, glens and lakes, valleys of shadow, ravines of black water, a land which God kneaded from a tough material and passed to man so that he might brawl on it with his fellow man because he couldn't brawl with rocks and heaths.

And this short letter is meant for you, Glasgow, city without beauty, city of noise and trade, city of factories and shipyards, harbour for all possible goods. What to say about you? Are factories beautiful then, docks and warehouses, cranes in the harbour, towers in the steelworks, herds of gasometers, rattling goods wagons,

tall chimneys and thundering steam hammers, constructions made of girders and iron, buoys in the water and mountains of coal? I, wretched sinner, both think and see that all of this is very beautiful and picturesque and grandiose but the life which is born of it, the streets, the people, the faces in the workshops and the typing pools, the people's homes, their children and their food, the life, my word, the life which maintains itself through these large and strong things is neither beautiful nor picturesque but has been forsaken by the breath of God, crude and dirty and sticky, noisy, smelly and oppressive, disorderly and cruel, crueller than hunger and more disorderly than destitution; and the fatigue of hundreds of thousands weighed upon me and I fled, Glasgow, because I didn't have the courage to look and compare.

THE LAKE DISTRICT

So that it might not be said that there are lakes only in Scotland, they are also in England, where they have as much as a whole district allotted to them: and Derwent Water is there and Bassenthwaite Lake, Wast Water and Thirlmere and Grasmere and Windermere and Ullswater and many others; and the Lake Poets lived here and Wordsworth has a small grave here in Grasmere next to a pretty old church with an oak ceiling in a valley of fuzzy trees; but although this sentence is so long, it hasn't included all the delights of this lovely, lake region. So, let us note that Keswick is a little town built unlike all other little towns in the world from pure, green stones; but because I don't have any green ink here I have at least drawn you the muni- cipal hall, which is also

111

pretty. For tourist reasons the mountain, Skiddaw, is here and later, between the groves and parks, the tender lake, Derwent Water, which I drew on such a sweet, silent evening that I was almost uneasy with joy.

The sunset combed the curly wavelets with a golden comb and here our pilgrim sat down above the quiet rushes and didn't want to go home, so intoxicating and tranquil is that water. The *Guide to the Lake District* identifies various mountains, passes and beautiful observation points and even a stone which Wordsworth often sat on and other local beauties. As for me, I discovered and undertook a few pilgrimages of my own:

1. *Pilgrimage to the Sheep*. It is true that there are sheep everywhere in England but lake sheep are particularly curly, graze on silken lawns and remind one of the souls of the blessed in heaven. No-one tends them and they spend their time in feeding, dreaming and pious contemplation. I have drawn them, investing

them with as much silent and gentle pleasure in life as it is possible to achieve with a fountain pen.

2. *Pilgrimage to the Cows*. Lake Cows differ from others in having a special, reddish tinge. Apart from

this, they are distinguished from other cows by the grace of the landscape in which they graze and the placidity of their expression. They stroll all day through elysian meadows and when they lie down they slowly and earnestly ruminate words of thanksgiving. I have surrounded them in my picture with all the beauties of the Lake Region. You can see a bridge there under which a little river flows full of trout, some silken bushes, fuzzy trees, oval and cozy wooded hills strewn with copses and hedgerows, ridges of Cumbrian mountains, and finally a sky full of moisture and light. Among clusters of trees you catch sight of the tops of houses made of slightly crimson or greenish stone and you recognise that to be a cow in the Lake District is a great priviledge which is bestowed on only the most saintly and dignified of all creatures.

3. *Pilgrimage to the Horses.* Horses in England do nothing else but graze all day or stroll over pretty

grass. Perhaps they aren't even horses but Swift's Houyhnhnms, a wise and semi-divine nation which doesn't engage in trade, abstains from politics and isn't even interested in the horse races at Ascot. They look on man benevolently and almost without antagonism; they are unusually reasonable. Some-times they contemplate, sometimes they run amok with their tails flying, and sometimes they look about so grandly and earnestly that a person feels like a monkey beside them. Drawing a horse is the most difficult task I have encountered until now. When I tried, the horses surrounded me and one of them tried with all his might to gobble up my sketchbook. I had to beat a retreat when he didn't want to be contented with my showing him my pictures from a distance.

* This is the horse which wanted to gobble up my sketchbook.

There is still a lot more which is beautiful in the Lake District: thus, in particular, winding rivers, ample and majestic trees, roads twisting like ribbons, the call of the mountains and the coziness of the valleys and the rippled and placid lakes. And charabancs full of tourists chug along these winding roads, cars fly along and women glide by on bicycles. Only the Sheep, Cows and Horses ruminate on the beauty of Nature deliberately and without haste.

NORTH WALES

Holy Writ states quite unmistakeably after all: 'Ac efe a ddywedodd hefyd wrth y bobloedd, Pan weloch gwm-mwl yn codi o'r gorllewin, yn y fan y dywedwch, Y mae cawod yn dyfod; ac felly y mae' (Luke XII.54). Although the Welsh Bible says this of the west wind, I set off in a west wind for Mount Snowdon or, more correctly, Eryri Y Wyddfa, so that I could see the whole of the Welsh land. Ac felly y mae: it not only rained but I found myself in the clouds and in such cold that on the crown of Snowdon I took shelter by a stove; a fire after all is very beautiful to look at and it is possible to think of scores of the finest things beside glowing coals. The guidebook praises the beauty and diversity of the view from Mount Snowdon; I saw heavy, white and grey clouds; I even felt them under my shirt. To the eye it isn't exactly ugly because it is white, but overly diverse it is not. Nevertheless, it was granted to me to set eyes on Lliwedd and Moel Offrwm and Cwm-y-Llan and Llyn Ffynnon-y-gwas and Crib-y-ddysgl; and tell me whether these beautiful names aren't worth a little drizzle, gales, cold weather and heavy cloud.

The ✻ ✻ Splendid View from the Top
of Snowdon

As far as the language of the Welsh is concerned, it is rather incomprehensible and, as my scholarly friend explained, also complicated. For example, a father is at one time called 'dad', at another 'tad' and at yet another 'nhad', depending on the circumstance. That it is a complicated language is evident from the fact that a village near Anglesey is called simply Llanfair-pwllgwyngyllgogerychwyrndrobwllllantysiliogogogoch. To let you know, Welsh Celtic sounds pretty, especially from the mouths of dark-haired girls who are almost French in type. Alas, old, Welsh women however wear men's caps. This is obviously a remnant of local folk costume, which in the case of women included an enormously high, men's top hat.

Otherwise, Wales isn't at all as strange and fearful as its place-names. One place is called Penmaenmawr and there are only quarries there and a seaside resort. I don't know why some names have a magical effect on me; I simply had to see Llandudno and I was broken-hearted: in the first place, it is pronounced differently and in the second, it is just a mass of hotels, rocks and sand, like any other seaside resort on this island. I also crept as far as Caernarvon, the main town of the Welsh. It is so far away that at the post office they haven't heard of our country and at seven o'clock you won't get any dinner; I don't know why I was there a whole two days. They have a vast, old castle for the Princes of Wales there; I would have drawn it but it didn't fit onto my paper; but I did at least draw one of its towers, where

an autonomous parliament of jackdaws was just in session. Never in all my life have I seen and heard so many jackdaws. I tell you, you must go to Caernarvon.

Wales is the land of mountains, Lloyd George, trout, hikers, black cows, slate, castles, rains, bards and the Celtic tongue. The mountains are bare and violet and strange and full of stones; in the hotels there are damp photographs of the organisers of singing contests, which are a sort of national speciality here; Welsh sheep have long tails; and even if you were to cut me into pieces that is all I know about North Wales. If this seems little to anyone, well, let him go to Caernarvon. Change at Bangor.

LETTERS ABOUT IRELAND

I

As a matter of fact, I wanted to write some letters from Ireland; it isn't even more than a few, miserable hours from here; why it is that I am not going isn't even entirely clear to me. I think it is the fault of the Irish question.

I put the Irish question to almost all the Englishmen, Scotsmen, Cymry and Gaels I met. I asked them what exactly I ought to see in Ireland and where I ought to head. It seems that they found this question somewhat unpleasant. They told me that I would be better off going to Oxford or Stratford or to the coast.

And this inflamed my curiosity all the more.

'Go to the north,' one advised me.

'Go to the west,' another advised me, somewhat unenthusiastically.

'Go to the south,' spake a third. 'I've never been there myself but if you want to go...'

II

Question: I'd like to take a look at Ireland. What do you think?
Answer: Ah, eh, eh, eh, oh, oh. Eh?
Question: What?
Answer: It isn't exactly calm there.
Question: Are things so bad?
Answer: Well, they're blowing bridges sky high; and when a train comes...
Question: Do they blow every train sky high?
Answer (rather uncertainly): No, not every train. Do you know what? Go to Belfast. It's almost the same as here there...

III

Mr. Shaw then advised only one place in Ireland. It is a little islet in the south whose name I have forgotten. Apparently, the people there have been very well preserved. Unfortunately, Mr. Shaw added, it is impossible to land on the island in question.

IV

All right, you will take a look there for yourself. You will buy a guidebook on Ireland, you will choose a few, pretty places and you will write some letters from Ireland.

Beginning in Glasgow, I wander round all the book-

shops, looking for a guidebook on Ireland. But the bookseller shakes his head gravely: no, he hasn't got a guidebook on Ireland. He has got a guidebook on Cornwall and the Dukeries, Snowdonia and the exhibition at Wembley, but as it happens absolutely nothing about Ireland, sorry, nothing at all. 'Our people don't go there.'

V

It is a few, miserable hours from here to Ireland; but, tell me, should I for no earthly reason cast off the terrible secret in which this country is enshrouded for me? I shall always look at the map of Ireland with fondness and pleasure: 'Lo, the land whose veil I never lifted.'

BACK IN ENGLAND

DARTMOOR

Well, I have seen everything; I have seen mountains and lakes, the sea, pastures and regions similar to gardens; it is only a proper, English forest that I haven't seen because here, if I may say so, they don't have a forest for all the trees. I even made for a place which is marked 'Dartmoor Forest' on the map; moreover, Dartmoor is, if I am not mistaken in my literary history, the region of the hound of the Baskervilles. During the journey I saw where the Hispaniola set off for Stevenson's Treasure Island; it is in Bristol, most probably by the bridge where that brig stood, smelling of oranges. Otherwise, there is absolutely nothing in Bristol, except a pretty church where at that moment there was some praying, a cathedral where at that moment too there were devotions with singing and preaching, and finally an old hospital where I drew a bearded caryatid, a chimera with a full beard, which for Bristol is quite interesting.

In Exeter the English Sunday descended on me, together with the rain. The Exeter Sunday is so thorough and sacred that even the churches are closed; and as for one's physical welfare, any wayfarer who is contemptuous of cold potatoes has to go to bed on an empty stomach; I don't know what particular pleasure the Exeter God derives from this. Otherwise, it is a pretty town with pleasant and quiet rain and old, English houses which I will come back to later because now I am hurrying to Dartmoor Forest.

One travels there along beautifully winding roads, across round hillocks, through that shaggily green region where there are the densest hedges, the largest sheep and the most ivy, copses and hawthorns and the bushiest trees and cottages covered with the thickest thatches that I have ever seen. An old tree like this in Devonshire is as compact as a rock and as perfect as a statue. Then come protracted, bare, desolate hills without a single tree: this is Dartmoor Forest. Here and there a raised, granite boulder protrudes on the heathy wilderness like the altar of some giants or primordial lizards. For the information, these are 'tors'. Sometimes a small, red stream runs through the heath, a sunken pool blackens, an overgrown fen flashes. It is said that a rider and his horse will sink in this without trace, but I couldn't try because I didn't have a horse. The low ridges cloud over (I don't know whether this is the falling of the dragging clouds or the steaming of the eternally oozing earth); a misty veil of rain envelops the region of granite and swamps, the clouds roll up densely and a dim, tragic light reveals for a moment a desolate heath of heather, juniper and bracken which was once a deep, impenetrable forest.

What is it in man when he sees such a region of dread and nostalgia that makes him catch his breath—is it because it is beautiful?

Up and down, up and down through green Devon, between two walls of a hedgerow which squares off the open countryside just as perfumed field borders do in our country, and always among old trees, among the wise eyes of the herds, up and down to the red coast of Devon.

PORTS

But of course, having been to look at some ports and having seen so many, I now confuse them. So wait: Folkestone, London, Leith and Glasgow: that's four; then Liverpool, Bristol, Plymouth and maybe there were even more. The nicest is Plymouth, which is prettily sunk among rocks and islands and where they have an old harbour in the Barbican with genuine sailors, fishermen and black skiffs and a new harbour under Hoe promenade with captains, statues and a striped lighthouse. I have drawn this lighthouse but you can't see that it is a pale, blue night, that the green and red lamps of the buoys and ships are sparkling on the sea, that I am

sitting under the lighthouse and have a black bird in my lap—I mean a real bird[†]—, that I am patting the sea, the bird, the little lights on the sea and the whole world in a preposterous fit of joy at being in the world; and below in the Barbican it reeks of fish and the ocean as it did in the time of old Drake and Captain Marryat and the sea is peaceful, wide and luminous. I tell you, Portsmouth is the prettiest port.

But Liverpool, folks, is the biggest; and because of its size I will now forgive it the wrong it did me, for, on account of some congress or royal visit or whatever it was, it didn't want to provide our wayfarer with a place to stay for the night and it terrified me with its new cathedral, as large and hopeless as the ruins of the baths of Caracalla in Rome, and was idle at midnight in the puritanical darkness so that I couldn't find my way to the wretched inn which had given me a damp

Liverpool

[†] Note: Čapek's word is 'kočka' (cat), which can have the same slang meaning as 'bird' or 'chick' in English.

couch smelling like a cask of cabbage—well, I forgive Liverpool for everything because there was something to see from Dingle up to Bootle and as far again as Birkenhead on the other side: yellow water, bellowing steam ferries, tugboats, pot-bellied, black sows rocking on the waves, white, transatlantic liners, docks, basins, towers, cranes, silos, elevators, smoking factories, stevedores, skiffs, warehouses, shipyards, barrels, chests, parcels, chimneys, masts, rigging, trains, smoke, chaos, hooting, ringing, hammering, puffing, the ruptured bellies of the ships, the stench of horses, of sweat, urine and waste from all the continents of the world; and if I heaped up words for another half an hour I wouldn't achieve the full number, confusion and expanse which is called Liverpool.

A steamer is beautiful when, hooting, it severs the water with its high breast, belching smoke from its chimneys; it is beautiful when it disappears beyond the arched shoulder of the waters, dragging a veil of smoke behind it; distance and destination are beautiful, man, as you stand on the prow and embark. A sailing ship is beautiful, gliding over the waves. To depart and to arrive are beautiful. My homeland which doesn't have a sea, isn't your horizon somewhat narrow and don't you lack the murmur of distant places? Yes, yes, but there can be humming areas around our heads; if it isn't possible to sail, it is at least possible to think, to furrow the wide and high world with wings of the spirit. I tell you, there is still enough space for expeditions and great ships. Yes, it is necessary to put out to sea continuously; the sea is everywhere where there is courage.

But, helmsman, please don't turn back; we aren't sailing home yet. Let us stay a while longer in this roadstead in Liverpool and look at everything before we go back; it is huge, dirty and noisy. Where actually is the real England? There in those quiet and clean cottages among the frightfully old trees and traditions, in the homes of perfect, peaceable and gentle people or here in these gloomy waves, in the hammering docks, in Manchester, Poplar or Glasgow's Broomielaw? Very well, I admit that I don't understand: there in that England it is almost too perfect and beautiful; and here it is almost too...

Very well, I don't understand; it is as if it weren't even one country and one nation. So be it, let's sail then; may the sea spray me; may the wind lash me; I think I have seen too much.

MERRY OLD ENGLAND

We must however pull up once more; we must just look to see where this merry old England actually is. Old England is, let us say, Stratford, it is Chester, Exeter and I don't know where else. Stratford, Stratford, hang on, have I been there? No, I haven't; and I haven't seen Shakespeare's parental home—if we ignore the fact that it has been rebuilt from the ground up and, besides this, that perhaps no such Shakespeare existed at all. But, on the other hand, I have been to Salisbury, where an entirely unquestionable Massinger worked, and to the Temple in London, where a guaranteed Dickens stayed, and to Grasmere, where a historically-substantiated Wordsworth lived, and to many other documentarily indisputable birthplaces and spheres of activity. Well then, here and there I found that good old England whose exterior consists of timbers and carvings, as a result of which it is striped in a pretty black and white. I wouldn't like to make overly bold hypotheses, but it seems to me that the black and white stripes on English policemen's sleeves have their direct origin in this striped style of old

English houses, as our picture shows.

England after all is a land of historical traditions; and everything that is, has some cause, as I believe John Locke taught. In some towns, as for example Chester, policemen wear white coats like surgeons or barbers; maybe this is a tradition from the time of the Romans. Besides this, old England delighted in all sorts of protruding storeys and gables, so that a house of this sort is always wider at the top. In addition, even the windows were usually thrust out like half-opened drawers, so that a house like this, with its storeys, oriels, projections and recesses, looks like a large, collapsible toy or an old

secretaire with drawers which perhaps tucks away and closes for the night and that's that. In Chester they have, moreover, what are called 'rows'. This is an arcade, but on the first floor, and it is reached from the street by stairs, so that the shops are both below and above. This exists nowhere else in the world. And in Chester they also have a cathedral made of pink stone, whereas in York the cathedral is brown, in Salisbury pike-blue and in Exeter black and green. Almost all English cathedrals have pillars in the style of pipes, a rectangular presbytery, an atrocious organ in the middle of the main nave and fan-shaped groins in a vaulted ceiling. What the Puritans didn't destroy, the deceased Wyatt finished off with his stylistically-pure renovations. For example, the cathedral in Salisbury is so hopelessly perfect that it makes you feel uneasy; and you circumambulate the city of Salisbury three times, as Achilles did the city of Troy, and afterwards, finding that you still have another two hours before your train departs, you sit on a bench in the town between three one-legged old men and watch as a local policeman puffs out his cheeks to make an infant laugh in its pram. On the whole, there is nothing more dreadful than when it rains in a small town.

In Salisbury they also have the walls of the houses covered in roofing tiles. I have drawn them in order to please the tiler, into whose hands perhaps this letter will fall. In the northern coun-

ties they have built houses of pretty, grey stones; this is the reason why almost all the houses in London are built of ugly, grey bricks. In Berkshire and Hampshire they have built everything of paprika-red bricks; that is why the streets in London are made of red brick, as if the angel of death had anointed them with blood. In Bristol a builder has made thousands of windows with strange, somewhat Moorish arches, and in Tavistock all the houses have a portal like Princetown prison. I am afraid that with this I have now exhausted the architectural diversity of England.

Most beautiful in England though are the trees, the herds and the people; and then the ships. Old England also means those pink old gentlemen who with the advent of spring wear grey top hats and in summer chase small balls over golf courses and look so hearty and amiable that if I were eight years old I would want to play with them and old ladies who always have knitting in their hands and are pink, beautiful and kind, drink hot water and never tell you about their illnesses.

On the whole, a country which has been able to create the most beautiful childhood and the most hearty old age certainly has something of the best in this vale of tears.

OUR PILGRIM NOTICES
THE PEOPLE

In England I would like to be a cow or a child; but, being an adult and overgrown man, I have taken a look at the people of this country. Well then, it isn't true that all Englishmen wear checked clothes and have a pipe and whiskers. As far as the latter is concerned, the only true Englishman is Dr. Bouček in Prague. Every Englishman has a raincoat or an umbrella, a flat cap and a newspaper in his hand. If it is an English-woman, she has a raincoat or a tennis racket. Nature has a predilection here for unusual shagginess, over-growth, bushiness, woolliness, bristliness and all types of hair. So, for example, English horses have whole tufts and tassels of hair on their legs, and English dogs are nothing but ridiculous bundles of locks. Only the English lawn and the English gentle-man are shaved every day.

What an English gentleman is, can't be said succinctly: at the very least you would have to know an English club waiter or a ticket clerk at a railway station or even a policeman. A gentleman is a restrained fusion of silence, willingness, dignity, sport, news-

HAIR

papers and propriety. For two hours the person opposite you on the train will exasperate you by not deeming you worthy of a glance; suddenly he will stand up and hand you your case, which you can't quite reach. Here people are always able to help each other but they never have anything to say to each other, unless it is about the weather. Maybe that is why Englishmen have devised so many games, because one doesn't talk while playing games. Their reticence is such that they don't even swear in public about the government, the train or taxes; on the whole, they are a joyless and reserved people. In place of pubs where one sits, drinks and chats, they have invented bars where one stands, drinks and remains silent. The more talkative people give themselves over to politics, like Lloyd George, or to authorship; an English book, to wit, has to have at least four hundred pages.

Perhaps it has come about from the selfsame reticence that the English swallow half of every word and the other half they somehow squash. Sharing an understanding with them is difficult too. Every day I travelled to the bus stop at Ladbroke Grove. The conductor comes and I say, 'Ledbrrook Grerv.' '...?? Eh?' 'Ledbhook Gerv!' 'Eh?' 'Hevhoov Hev!' 'Ah, Hevhoov Hov,' the conductor rejoices and gives me a ticket to Ladbroke Grove. I will never learn this as long as I live.

But if you get to know them closer, they are very dear and gentle. They never talk much because they never talk about themselves. They amuse themselves like children but with the gravest, leathery expressions. They have a great deal of ingrained etiquette but at the same time they are as spontaneous as puppies. They are as hard as flint, incapable of adjusting themselves, conservative, loyal, a little shy and always uncommunicative. They can't step out of their skin, but it is a solid and in every respect excellent skin. You can't talk to them without them inviting you to lunch or dinner; they are as hospitable as St. Julian, but they are never able to overcome the distance between man and man. Sometimes it makes you uneasy how lonely you can feel in the midst of these kindly and willing people; but if you were a little boy you would know that you can trust them more than yourself and you would be freer and held in more respect than anywhere in the world; a policeman would puff out his cheeks to make you laugh, an old gentleman would play ball with you and a white-haired lady would lay down her four-hundred-page novel to look prettily at you with her bluish-grey and still young eyes.

A FEW FACES

But I have still a few faces here which I must give and describe.

This is Mr. Seton-Watson or Scotus Viator. You all know him because he fought for us like the archangel

Gabriel. He has a house on the Isle of Skye, is writing a history of the Serbs and in the evening plays the pianola by a hearth burning with peat. He has a beautiful, tall wife, two waterproof boys and a blue-eyed baby, windows onto the sea and the islands, a childish mouth and rooms full of ancestors and pictures of Czechoslovakia; a delicate and hesitant man, far subtler of face than you would expect from this strict and just, Scottish pilgrim.

This is Mr. Nigel Playfair, a man of the theatre. He is the gentleman who introduced my plays to England, but he does even better things; he is a level-headed

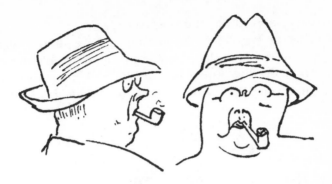

person, an artist, entrepreneur and one of the few truly modern producers in England.

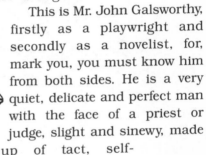

This is Mr. John Galsworthy, firstly as a playwright and secondly as a novelist, for, mark you, you must know him from both sides. He is a very quiet, delicate and perfect man with the face of a priest or judge, slight and sinewy, made up of tact, self-restraint and contemplative shyness, and enormously serious; only around his eyes is there a smile of kindly, attentively folded wrinkles. He has a wife who is very similar to him and his books are the perfect and wise works of a sensitive and rather sad observer.

This is Mr. G. K. Chesterton. I have drawn him flying, in the first place because I was only able to get a rather fleeting impression of him and then because of his heavenly exuberance. Unfortunately, at that

moment he was probably rather depressed by a slightly official situation: he could only manage a smile, but his smile has the strength of three others. If I could write about his books, his poetic democracy and his genial optimism, it would be the merriest of my letters, but because I have taken it into my head to write only about what I have seen with my own eyes I will describe for you an ample gentleman whose spatial proportions remind one of Viktor Dyk. He has a musketeer moustache and shy, intelligent eyes beneath pince-nez, awkward hands, as fat people often have, and a fluttering tie; he is at once a child, a giant, a curly lamb and an aurochs; he has a large, russet head with a pensive and whimsical expression and at first sight he aroused a bashfulness in me and intense attachment; I didn't see him again.

And this is Mr. H. G. Wells, firstly as he appears among people and secondly as he appears at home; a massive head, strong, broad shoulders and strong, warm palms. He looks like a farmer, a working man, a father and everything in the world. He has the thin and hazy voice of a man who is no public speaker, a face inscribed with thought and work, a harmonious home, a pretty, petite wife who is as chipper as a redpoll, two, large, playful boys and eyes that look  as if they were half-closed and veiled beneath strong, English eyebrows. Simple and reasonable, healthy, strong, well-informed and very ordinary in every good and vital sense of the word. A person forgets that he is speaking to a great author because he is speaking to a level-headed and universal man. The best of health to you, Mr. Wells.

This is an almost supernatural personality, Mr. Bernard Shaw. I couldn't draw him better because he  is always moving and talking. He is immensely tall, thin and straight and looks half like God and half like a very malicious satyr, who, however, by a thousand-year process of sublimation has lost everything that is too natural. He has white hair, a white beard and very pink skin, inhumanly clear eyes, a strong and pugnacious nose, something knightly from Don Quixote, something apostolic and something which makes fun of everything in the world, including himself; never in all my life have I seen such an unusual being; to tell you the truth, I was frightened of him. I thought that it was some spirit which was only playing at being the celebrated Bernard Shaw. He is a vegetarian, I don't know whether from principle or from gourmandaise. One never knows whether people have principles on principle or whether for their own personal satisfaction. He has a level-headed wife, a quiet spinet and windows onto the Thames; he sparkles with life and has a great many interesting things to say about himself, Strindberg, Rodin and other famous things; to listen to him is joy combined with awe.

I ought to draw a lot more striking and beautiful heads which I met. They were men, women and pretty girls, men of letters, journalists, students, Indians, scholars, club men, Americans and everything which exists in the world; but we must say goodbye, friends; I don't want to believe that I have seen you for the last time.

ESCAPE

To end, I will divulge some terrible things. For example, the English Sunday is frightful. People say that Sunday exists so that one can travel to the country. This isn't true: people travel to the country to protect themselves in wild panic from the English Sunday. On Saturday a gloomy instinct to flee somewhere seizes every Briton, just as wild animals in gloomy instinct flee an approaching earthquake. Anyone who can't escape repairs at least to a church so that he can ride out the dreadful day in prayers and song. A day when no-one cooks, travels, looks or thinks. I don't know for what inexpressible wrongs the Lord has sentenced England to the weekly punishment of Sunday.

English cuisine is of two kinds: good and middling. Good English cooking is simply French cooking. Middling cuisine in a middling hotel for a middling Englishman to a large extent explains the English gloominess and reticence. No-one can radiate and warble chewing pressed beef smeared with diabolical mustard. No-one can rejoice out loud, unsticking trembling tapioca pudding from his teeth. A man becomes terribly serious if he gets salmon doused in pink dextrin; and if he has something for breakfast, lunch and dinnner which, while living is a fish and in a melancholy state of edibility is called 'fried sole', if he has tanned his stomach three times a day with black, leather tea and has drunk gloomy, warm beer, if he has partaken of universal sauces, preserved vegetables, custard and mutton, well, he has probably exhausted all the bodily enjoyments of the average Englishman and begins to comprehend his reservedness, earnestness and strict morals. By contrast, toast, grilled cheese and grilled bacon are certainly the inheritance of merry old England. I am convinced that old Shakespeare didn't pour tannin tea down his throat and old Dickens didn't make the most of life over tinned beef. As for old John Knox, I am not so sure.

English cuisine lacks a certain lightness and floridity, a joy of life, melodiousness and sinful hedonism. I would say that English life lacks this too. The English street isn't voluptuous. Normal, average life isn't intermixed with cheerful noises, scents and spectacles. A normal day doesn't sparkle with pretty accidents, smiles and the budding of events. You can't merge with the streets, people and voices. Nothing winks at you friendlily and openly.

Lovers love one another gravely in parks, sternly and without a word. Drinkers drink in bars, each to himself. The average person travels home and reads his newspaper without looking to left or right. At home he has a fireplace, a small garden and the inviolable

privacy of his family. Besides this, he cultivates sport and the weekend. More about his life I have been unable to ascertain.

The Continent is noisier, less disciplined, dirtier, more rabid, craftier, more passionate, more convivial, more amorous, hedonistic, vivacious, coarse, garrulous, unruly and somehow less perfect. Please, give me a ticket straight to the Continent.

ON BOARD THE SHIP

A person on the shore would want to be on board the ship which is drawing away; a person on board the ship would want to be on the shore which is in the distance. When I was in England I thought constantly of what was beautiful at home. When I am at home I will think perhaps of what is higher and better in England than anywhere else.

I have seen greatness and power, wealth, prosperity and incomparable development. I was never sad that we are a small and unfinished part of the world. To be small, unsettled and uncompleted is a good and courageous mission. There are great and sumptuous, Atlantic liners with three funnels, a first class, bathrooms and polished brass, and there are small, smoking steamboats which rattle over the high seas. It takes quite a fair pluck, folks, to be such a small and uncomfortable banger. And don't say that conditions in our country are poor. The universe around us is, thank heaven, just as great as the universe around the British Empire. A small steamer doesn't hold as much as a large ship like this; but ha-ha, my friend, it can sail just as far, or somewhere else. It depends on the crew.

Everything is still ringing in my head; it takes a while, as when a person comes out of a vast factory and is deafened by the silence outside; and a moment more, as if all the church bells in England were still ringing:

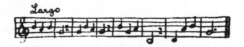

But the Czech words which I will shortly hear are already blending in. We are a small nation and so it will seem to me as though I know everyone personally. The first person I see will be a rotund and noisy person with a Virginia cigar, a person declaring some dissatisfaction, choleric, irritated, garrulous and wearing his heart upon his sleeve. And, praise God, it will be as if we know each other.

That low, narrow strip on the horizon is Holland already, with its windmills, avenues and black-and-

white cows; an even, pretty, people's country, cordial and comfortable.

Ik zal nog eens terugkomen

The white coast of England meanwhile has disappeared; shame: I forgot to say goodbye. But when I am at home, I will mull over everything that I have seen and when there will be talk of something, of the bringing up of children, of transportation, literature or the respect of man for man, of horses or armchairs, of what people are like or what they ought to be like, I will begin to say like an expert, 'Now, in England...'

But no-one will be listening to me.

THE END

YOU ENGLISH

[Karel Čapek writing for the *Daily Herald*]

In my younger years I was aware of only two types of Englishman. One was called John Bull; he was stout and ruddy, wore riding boots and breeches and was usually accompanied by a bulldog. The other was called Mr. Smith or something similar; he was tall and bony, wore checked clothes and red whiskers and was distinguished by the fact that he put his feet on the table at every possible opportunity. Both occurred mainly in burlesques and comedies.

When I later arrived in England, I found to my disappointment that the overwhelming majority of Englishmen do not wear checked clothes or whiskers or put their feet on tables and that (with the exception of Mr. G. B. Shaw) they are neither conspicuously tall nor (with the exception of Mr. G. K. Chesterton) conspicuously plump. Thus man loses the illusions of his youth. On the other hand, I discovered that England differs from the Continent in almost everything, beginning with grass and ivy and finishing with university or parliament. I could write in great detail about what distinguishes Notting Hill from Seville, but

I would be at a loss if I had to write about what universally and without exception distinguishes the inhabitants of the star called England from the inhabitants of the star called Europe. There is certainly a large difference as to the customs and standard of living of the average Briton and, let us say, a Macedonian shepherd; but I think that almost equally striking is the difference between the average Briton from the House of Lords and a Briton from the Isle of Dogs. I am not sure whether both of these classes of Briton have the same national qualities and the same national faults. I could write a treatise on the merits of Englishmen as far as I have observed them at The Athenaeum or on their unpleasant sides as far as I have observed them as tourists in Italy; but I realise that neither The Athenaeum, nor the whole of Italy, even including Sicily and the Riviera, are yet the whole of England.

I have been given the flattering invitation to tell the English to their attentive faces and from the heart everything that one might reproach them and their country for. Well then, I have found certain gloomy experiences in my memory, such as the English Sunday, English cuisine, English pronunciation and some other, utterly English customs; but I say to my-self, if the English indulge in these and similar matters, what business is it of us other nations? Why should I make excuses for their horrible custom of eating tapioca pudding or revere the English nobility? I have a special fondness for all manner of national customs, whether they be the customs of islanders from Fiji or of islanders from Great Britain. I would be delighted if Scottish bankers walked about in kilts with bare knees and playing bagpipes, or if Britons in the Savoy Hotel danced a sword dance instead of the foxtrot. I am inclined to regard all national peculiarities as a positive enrichment of this world. I admire England in particular for managing to maintain so many of its customs; I think that to these belong, for example, not only national pride but also a marked sense of humour. On the whole, the natives of the British Isles are more picturesque to foreign eyes than they themselves perhaps know. Barely any nation is as likeable as the English—with one condition: that you go to see them in their England. There you will fall for their customs, their restrained willingness, their formality and simplicity and a hundred other aspects of their British life. Only an insular nation could develop so many characteristic and enduring attributes. The greatest merit of the Britons is their insularity. But their insularity is also their greatest fault.

As long as the English are isolated in England, that is their business; rather worse is that they are isolated wherever they find themselves in the world. I have seen British isles and islets in France and Spain, in Italy and even in our country. This nation of seafarers, travellers and colonists cannot step outside England, it takes her with it, whether it travels to the equator or the North Pole. It can never draw nearer to other nations and their life. It is cosmopolitan so long as there are English-speaking waiters in this universe, English golf courses, English breakfast and, as far as possible, English society. It keeps almost scrupulously to one side if it lives in the midst of another nation. It is true that it hangs about its pictures and architecture and climbs up its highest mountains, but it does not take part in its life, it does not accept its joys, and cannot meet it on its own ground. In England even a foreigner can comprehend that within this psychological insularity there is a sturdy custom of not opening up and a certain diffidence; but abroad these typical, British traits easily begin to resemble pride, distrust and an egoistical reserve.

Well, even if that were the way that it was, it would be a purely private affair of the English themselves; but it ceases to be a private trait if British foreign policy also displays itself to foreign nations in a similar light. The nations of this planet can very often appraise British politics as being loyal, honourable, nay, even full of goodwill; but hardly ever can one shake off the impression that something is lacking: that 'something' might be called liking. British politics is global because the British Empire is global, not because British mentality is global. British politics recognises certain ideals because British moral law leads to them and not because some universal moral law leads to them. Sometimes England gives us others a helping hand like a true British gentleman; this does not happen so that she can act like a neighbour. I have observed that the English have a beautiful sense of friendship, but it seems that they are only friends amongst themselves. It is extremely easy to love them as long as we are living in England or reading English books, that is, as long as we are standing physically or spiritually on British soil; but it is somewhat more difficult to make friends with them while we are standing on a point in whatever other nation on this planet: precisely because they themselves, as it seems, do not stand on such things. Judge for yourselves whether this is a mistake of yours; perhaps it is—at least from a British point of view—your national prerogative.

A SPEECH FOR
BRITISH RADIO

My dear, British listeners,

Although I won't give this speech myself, I feel as I'm writing it a certain hesitation in front of you. It seems to me that it wouldn't be decent to say whatever I wanted against you, because you can't defend yourselves; you can't interrupt me and protest that I'm wrong. True, you could turn me off or conceivably take up a hammer and smash your wireless; still, some waves (or whatever they are) would flit across space, delivering false information about the islanders of Great Britain. Besides this, I'm a foreigner and have only been to England once, so I ask you not to consider me as an expert who knows more about England than others, but only as a foreigner who has been surprised by things in England which you are not surprised by.

I say I've only been to England once. That's not entirely true. Everyone who reads English Literature steps into the truest and most English England. If I understand, English Literature is even more English than the Church of England or English politics. I'd say that your books are as completely English as the

English countryside or the English family. Nothing more perhaps need be said in praise of your literature.

It appears that the islanders of Great Britain have long lived and continue to live under a peculiar delusion. They travel over the whole world imagining that the basin of the Niger or the Amazon is more romantic or more picturesque than, for example, the area around the river Cam. I was once introduced to a gentleman in London. 'How do you do,' he said affably, 'Have you been to China?' At the time I didn't try to explain to him that my thoughts weren't on China because at that moment I was discovering England and that to my mind England was just as exotic a country as China. It's not impossible that that gentleman is listening to my talk at this moment. I'd like to tell him that since that time I may not have been to China but I have been to several other interesting countries and none of them have been as strange and surprising as the Great National Reservation of the Anglo-Saxons and Caledonians through which I was then wandering. No country has preserved more of its original countryside and its tribal customs than England. I've met wayfaring Englishmen, for example, in Seville, Girgenti or Perugia; wherever they are, they take a piece of England with them in their customs and thinking, just as a bedouin takes his prayer mat with him, and they can't step outside her. I rather suspect that this is how the British Empire came into being: that some Briton landed on an unknown shore and established a golf course there, the English

Sunday, trade, hot water and a house with a brick fireplace. Wherever an Englishman stops, a British isle comes into being. Wayfaring Englishmen are wandering British isles. Sometimes this also counts for British politics, but that, as Mr. Kipling says, is another story.

If I should name a few things which strike the foreigner in your country as being especially English and consequently exceedingly picturesque, I would begin immediately with the ground you walk on. I remember the white chalk of Dover and red rocks in Devon, the pink granite of Inverness, the green stone of the Lake District and the blue slate of North Wales, or the black, brown, russet and red, lead-like bricks which old houses are built from in your old countryside. If anyone tries to tell me that England isn't as colourful as the Orient, I'll advise him to take a look at the English earth. I think that a nation born on earth which is so rich in colour can never grow old from a lack of imagination.

The second great impression which the pilgrim encounters in England is English turf, for not only is it as green and dense as no other turf in the world but one may walk over it. I suppose England became a land of freedom because it was permitted to tread on the grass there. Perhaps that's also why England has had so few revolutions in history: because Britons could always satisfy their instinct for freedom by a mere striding over the meadows. Nor do I consider it impossible that Britain began to rule the waves because she saw something in them like a great lawn over which it was permitted to proceed wherever one pleased. However this may be, for a Continental man, English lawns are a great experience.

A third, robust impression is made by English trees. They are, after all, unusually old and large and a pilgrim discovers through them that old things can be truly living. There are old trees everywhere but in England there are almost only old trees. A botanist explained to me that their particular amplitude has something to do with the English climate, but I think that it has more to do with the English predilection for old and venerable things such as tradition, the House of Lords, Oxford colleges and so on. I think that a tree in England grows from the outset to become an ancient and ample tree, as dignified as a cathedral. It seems to me that England is a country where even people have discovered the secret of how to grow old beautifully and with dignity. If a Continental person wants to address someone or something especially tenderly he employs a diminutive and describes the cherished things as being 'small'; but an Englishman calls them 'dear old'. In England there are many things which are held in great esteem not because they're useful but because they're old. I'd say that the English live in a deeper and more expansive time than other, less conservative nations; in their present tense there are both present and past ages. When I saw English lawyers for the first time in periwigs (which was in Edinburgh) I understood one of the secrets of English traditionalism, namely a sense of humour. It's a greater joke if someone wears a periwig from the eighteenth century than if he wears an ordinary and unhistorical, bald patch. In many cases it seems that your ability to preserve old traditions flows from your goodwill not to spoil a joke.

Well then, I could continue—beginning with geological composition and vegetation—about the peculiarities of England; I could rise in stages of creation to higher and higher beings, to cows and sheep, horses and dogs and the special status with which they are blessed in England, until I reached the highest sphere in which there are children, clubs, colleges, gentlemen, butlers and London policemen. I make bold to say that no exotic ethnography abounds in more remarkable phenomena than normal, English life. The war dances of Central Borneo aren't one jot more interesting than English sports. Indian fakirs aren't more fantastical than the speakers in Hyde Park Corner. Abraham's family life couldn't have been more patriarchal than the English weekend. Secret associations of African natives aren't more ritualistic than English clubs. As you see, I'm speaking only of more or less public phenomena; it's possible to suppose that besides these there are a great many English customs of a more private character which no highly scholarly professor has yet collated and scrutinised.

I'll linger on the peculiarities of the British islanders in order to emphasise the particular insularity of the English character. There are travellers who consider England a part of Europe and others who regard her as an island. As for me, I'd rather say that England is a world of her own. Evidently only for reasons of stringency (for the universe, as Einstein and Eddington teach us, is infinite), England wasn't created a separate planet, but this could have been quite fine for her. She could have been a mysterious land in an unknown sea which only a shipwrecked sailor could reach by accident, driven there by a storm. Having then returned like Gulliver from his travels, he'd perhaps tell his Continental listeners this:

'When I'd been driven by the sea-storm for nine days and nine nights I saw a coast a hundred feet high, white and flush like the wall of a house or rampart. Once I'd ascended the rock I found a great park above. There are no fields there or woods or vineyards and they don't cultivate corn or turnip as in our country but only lawns and trees, as in a park. In this park, called England, there live people who are by and large similar to us Europeans; they have houses with high chimneys but around these houses there aren't any railings or walls as in our country which might bar access to strangers but only a tablet on which is written a potent and magical word.'

'Which word?' the listeners would ask.

'The word 'Private',' the adventurer would continue. 'In this country that word has such a magical power that it replaces railings and ramparts. Afterwards, I got into a train and travelled to the capital. A man sat in the carriage with me but he didn't look at me and he didn't enter into conversation with me in the least and he didn't begin to ask where I was going and what I wanted there.'

'That's not possible,' the Continental listeners would clamour. 'What, was this man dumb?'

'No,' the adventurer would say, 'but in this country people have a custom of being silent and they don't like to become acquainted. But when I wanted to get out of the train the man stood up and helped me with my luggage, without speaking to me or even only looking at me.'

'This is a strange people,' the listeners would surmise.

'It is,' the seafarer would say, 'but if you keep interrupting me I'll never be finished. This capital is the largest city in area in the world. In the middle of the city there is a great lawn called 'Hyde Park' and sheep graze there as in the country. There too anyone who wants to can stand up and preach whatever faith he wants. No-one will forbid him and no-one will laugh at him. There are many millions of people there and no-one will interfere in another person's business. I saw two drunkards brawling in the street; a policeman stood above them but he didn't interfere with them and he didn't disperse them; he only looked on to see that their fight was fair. When I'd learnt a little of the language of these islanders, I found that they don't usually say 'it's raining' or 'two and two are four' but 'I think it's raining', 'I rather think that two and two are four', and so on. It's as if they continuously and deliberately leave the other person the freedom to be of another opinion. I've even noticed that everyone is free to run across the grass there.'

At this the Continental listeners wouldn't be able to restrain themselves any longer and would say to the adventurer, 'Mr. Čapek, you are an enormous liar!'

*

I'm not a liar. I could go on and list a thousand and one differences between English and Continental life, between the mores, customs, practises and manners in our country and in yours, but I realise that in so doing I wouldn't do justice to what is most characteristic about England. England after all is a country of antonyms. It is the most beautiful and at the same time the ugliest of all the countries I've ever seen. It has developed the most appalling, modern industrialism and at the same time has preserved the most original, bucolic life. It is the most democratic of all nations and at the same time holds the oldest, most outdated remnants of aristocracy in esteem. It is at once puritanically serious and childishly gay. It possesses the most tolerance and at the same time the most prejudices. It is the most international of all countries and despite this the least bereft of local and provincial feelings and interests. Its inhabitants are unusually timid and at the same time unusually self-confident. They combine within themselves the maximum of personal freedom and the maximum of loyalty. English life is woven from sober 'common sense' and the irrationalism of Alice's Wonderland. And so on. England is a land of paradoxes; that's why it continues to be a land of mystery.

*

But it's time that I got to the core of the matter. This England, this old, paradoxical, particularist, insular, English England, in short, this Great Britain of yours, isn't the whole England. Wherever in the world you see a parliament, you see a piece of England, for England gave birth to parliamentarianism. Wherever you encounter political democracy, you discover a piece of English spiritual territory, for England was the first in our world to define the ideals of democracy. And wherever on this planet ideals of personal freedom and dignity apply, of tolerance, respect for the individual and inviolable human rights, there you will find the cultural inheritance of England, and you won't be looking at foreign lands but at the Greater England which is the home of most civilised people. Well then, every fight for the preservation of democracy is at the same time a fight for this Greater England, this spiritual empire which extends far beyond the borders of Great Britain. This fight, or more peaceably said, this development of the world, will decide the fate of certain principles, values and ideals in which the spirit of England has made itself manifest; today it really does come down to their preservation or extinction. I'd say that the English coast begins wherever the virtues of freedom apply. In this world there are many Dovers, but you must search for them on the moral map of the world.

I hope that with these reflections I won't overstep the theme which was set for me. If you have the patience to hear how a foreign pilgrim looks on England, allow him at the same time to think of the wider area which has also been formed by England, of the spirit of the West which wouldn't have been born without England. I like England as much for her individuality as for her universality. Someone once asked me which country I like most. I told him, 'The best scenery I've seen is in Italy; the best life I've observed is in France; the best people I've met are in England; but I can only live in my own country.' Well then, not many of you know the country in which I'm thinking of you. Three hundred years ago your Shakespeare had sweet Perdita shipwrecked on the Czech coast. It was partly a mistake and partly premature. We don't have a coast and only in present times can we say with a certain right: 'We too are Dover and our borders are the cliffs of the West.'

EXPLANATORY NOTES

Many people and many sources have contributed to create these notes and it would be impossible to thank or record them all here individually, as I would like. However, Otakar Vočadlo's *Anglické listy Karla Čapka* (Academia, 1975) has been particularly useful.

Letters from England: According to Vočadlo, Čapek's title was suggested by Roman Dyboski, a Polish colleague of Vočadlo at the School of Slavonic Studies in London. However, Čapek had already published impressions of a journey around Italy called *Letters from Italy* in 1923.

ENGLAND

FIRST IMPRESSIONS

p. 23   *the master, Chauliac:* Léon Chauliac: a destitute French artist whom Čapek and his brother, Josef, had befriended in Paris in 1911. Chauliac's spontaneous paintings and naive attitude to the world as a subject for art and as a source of beauty filled Josef in particular, who was an artist in his own right, with great enthusiasm. Karel Čapek devoted a study, *The*

Unknown Master, to Chauliac in 1921.

p. 25   *While I was still in Holland*: Čapek had wanted to visit Holland on his way to Britain. Instead, he travelled direct to London via Vlissingen (Flushing).

p. 26   *a good, Czech, guardian angel*: Otakar Vočadlo. In a letter to Vočadlo on 24th May, 1924 Čapek had hoped that Vočadlo would meet him at Victoria Station 'like a helping angel'.

p. 26   *Surbiton*: Vočadlo lived at 33, Adelaide Road. Čapek stayed with him and his family for the first days of his stay in Britain, frequently visited at the week-ends, returned there with Vočadlo at the end of their tour and also wrote parts of *Letters from England* there.

LONDON STREETS

p. 31   *this miserable road in Notting Hill*: Ladbroke Grove, where Čapek stayed after his first few days with the Vočadlos and after a short stay at Berner's Hotel as the guest of P.E.N. He stayed in Ladbroke Grove with a Czech, Mrs. Brown, who was the widow of a London policeman. According to Vočadlo, Capek may have been attracted to stay in Notting Hill after reading G. K. Chesterton's *The Napoleon of Notting Hill* (1904).

TRAFFIC

p. 37   *Antaeus*: the son of Poseidon. Antaeus was invincible as long as he remained in contact with his mother, Earth. Herakles therefore crushed him by lifting him off the ground.

HYDE PARK

Hyde Park as a symbol of democracy has continued to fascinate Czechs and Slovaks. Without a doubt, Čapek's account has contributed to this fascination. During the Prague Spring of 1968, when Czechoslovaks tried to achieve greater freedom under communist rule, the term 'hydepark' was coined as a name for the new, informal, open-air discussions.

AT THE NATURAL HISTORY MUSEUM

p. 45   *the Wallace Collection*: Sir Richard Wallace (1818-90) was an art connoisseur who bequeathed his art collection to his wife, who in turn bequeathed it to the British nation. The collection was first exhibited publicly in 1900 and is especially well-known for its eighteenth-century French paintings, furniture and porcelain.

p. 45   *Queen Mab*: in British folklore, queen of the fairies. She is also a recurrent figure in English Literature, most obviously in Shelley's *Queen Mab*, which was published in 1813. Čapek greatly admired Shelley, once describing him as 'one of the most noble-minded spirits in world poetry'. He also directed one of the world's first productions of Shelley's *The Cenci* in Prague in September 1922.

p. 46   *netsuke*: an ornamental pendant worn suspended from a girdle on a Japanese man's kimono. It is traditionally made of lacquered wood, horn, shell, jade, amber or porcelain.

OUR PILGRIM SIFTS THROUGH OTHER MUSEUMS

This is almost certainly an allusion to the writing of Jan Amos Komenský (1592-1670) and particularly to his greatest Czech work, *The Labyrinth of the World and Paradise of the Heart* (1623), which is narrated by a pilgrim and has chapter headings in the same style. Komenský was one of the most distinguished and influential Czechs of all time. He was a tireless educational and social reformer, religious leader, patriot and internationalist. He believed in 'natural' methods of learning and in the power of education to enlighten, advance and unite humanity. His ideas, particularly after his stay in England from 1641 to 1642, were influential in the founding of the Royal Society. Throughout his tragic life, which included exile and death abroad at the beginning of what were to be centuries of Hapsburg religious and political domination of his country, he was a staunch defender of the rights of his people. When Čapek wrote *Letters from England* in 1924, Komenský was especially present in Czechoslovaks' minds because the foundation of the independent Czechoslovak Republic only six years before had finally seemed to fulfil Komenský's famous prophesy: 'I too trust the Almighty that once the tempest of wrath hath passed... thy sovereign rule shall return to thee, my Czech people' (*Testament of the Dying Mother of the Community of Brethren*, 1650). Čapek's allusion to Komenský is also a humorous indication of his sense of himself in the modern labyrinth of Britain.

p. 49   *Yucatan*: a peninsula in South America, most of it in Mexico and parallel with Cuba.

p. 50   *Nineveh*: the capital of the Assyrian Empire from the 8th century B.C. until it was destroyed in 612 B.C. It is located opposite modern Mosul in northern Iraq.

OUR PILGRIM SEES
ANIMALS AND FAMOUS PEOPLE

p. 54   *King Alfonso*: King Alfonso XIII of Spain (1886-1941) was married to a granddaughter of Queen Victoria, Princess Victoria of Battenberg. He survived several assassination attempts, not least on his wedding day. By the time of Čapek's visit to Madame Tussaud's, Alfonso had experienced thirty-three different governments in twenty-one years. Alfonso refused to abdicate but was forced into exile and died in Rome in 1941. Madame Tussaud's removed his waxwork figure before his death, in 1934.

p. 54   *Mademoiselle Lenglen*: Suzanne Lenglen (1899-1938) was six times Wimbledon champion, a double Olympic gold medallist (Antwerp, 1920) and lost only one match in her entire amateur lawn tennis career.

p. 55   *Arthur Devereux*: his victims, in fact, were his wife and children, whom he concealed in a trunk and moved from place to place.

CLUBS

John Galsworthy invited Čapek to The Athenaeum where he met, among others, G. B. Shaw and A. A. Milne and where he was granted honorary membership during his stay in London. The Bone brothers (see note to p. 88) invited him to the Caledonian Club, where he met Arnold Bennett. He was also invited to the Albermarle Club by R. W. Seton-Watson (see note to p. 138) and took part in a discussion at The Student Movement House in Russell Square.

p. 56   *Herbert Spencer* (1820-1903): a self-educated sociologist and philosopher who was also sub-editor of *The Economist* from 1848 to 1853. Spencer believed in a form of evolution before Darwin and first coined the phrase 'the survival of the fittest'. He is particularly well-known for his belief that all development in the universe is a movement from homogeneity to heterogeneity, an idea which is central to his ten-volume *Synthetic Philosophy*.

p. 57   *F. Götz*: František Götz (1894-1974) was a literary and theatre critic, theorist, playwright, scriptwriter and novelist. Between 1923 and 1944 he taught drama theory and was later artistic director at the National Theatre in Prague. After 1945 he founded the Czechoslovak Academy of the Performing Arts where he also taught.

p. 57   *Zákrejs*: František Zákrejs (1839-1907) was a novelist, playwright and critic for the cultural magazine, *Osvěta*.

p. 57   *Šrámek*: Fraňa Šrámek (1877-1952) was a poet, prose writer and playwright. He was one of Čapek's closest friends and was one of the early circle of writers and other personalities who met at Čapek's home on Fridays from the autumn of 1924.

p. 57   *Šmilovský*: Alois Vojtěch Šmilovský (1837-1883), properly Alois Schmillauer. Šmilovský was a novelist and short story writer who also wrote tales from the life of the Czech philologist, Josef Dobrovský.

p. 57   *Professor Rádl*: Emanuel Rádl (1873-1942) was a philosopher and biologist and the author of *A History of Biological Theory from the End of the Seventeenth Century* (1905) and of *A History of Philosophy* (1931-2).

p. 58   *Hattala*: Martin Hattala (1821-1903) was Professor of Slovak Philology at Charles University in Prague and author of the first systematic grammar of Slovak.

THE BIGGEST SAMPLES FAIR OR THE GREAT BRITISH EMPIRE EXHIBITION

The British Empire Exhibition: the British Empire Exhibition was held at the new Wembley (or 'Empire') Stadium. Čapek visited it on 2nd June, 1924.

p. 63   *Wenceslas Square*: in Czech, *Václavské náměstí*, named after sv. Václav (St. Wenceslas), the patron saint of the Czechs. The square is in fact a long boulevard and is a traditional public meeting-place at times of great national importance such as the foundation of the Czechoslovak Republic in 1918, the invasion of Czechoslovakia by Warsaw Pact troops in 1968 and the Velvet Revolution in 1989.

p. 64   *Flying Scotsman*: Čapek was particularly keen to see the *Flying Scotsman* and travelled on it on 1st July, 1924.

p. 66   *Śākyamunis*: Śākyamuni is a Sanskrit name for the Indian nobleman more generally known as Buddha.

Literally, it means 'the sage of the Śākya', the Śākya being the tribe into which Buddha was born.

p. 67   *the extinct emu*: the common emu or *Dromaius novaehollandiae* is the sole surviving emu, the others having been exterminated by Australian settlers.

p. 67   *old Prouza*: Mr. Kristian Prouza.

p. 67   *Úpice*: a small town in north Bohemia, north of Hradec Králové and close to the Polish border. Čapek was born in Malé Svatoňovice, two and a half miles north-west of Úpice. Čapek's family moved to Úpice after his birth and he received his first schooling there.

THE EAST END

p. 69   *Košíře*: a western suburb of Prague.

THE COUNTRY

p. 74   *down in Surrey and up in Essex*: Čapek stayed with James Bone (see note to p. 88) in Guildford, Surrey and with H. G. Wells at Easton Glebe, Essex.

CAMBRIDGE AND OXFORD

p. 79   *eating on a dais*: Čapek was invited to dine at High Table at King's College, Cambridge by the physicist, P. M. S. Blackett (1897-1974). Blackett was awarded a Nobel Prize in 1948, was President of the Royal Society between 1965 and 1970 and became a life peer in 1969.

p. 79   *at the Half-Moon*: Čapek and Vočadlo stayed with Vočadlo's friend, Noel Porter, at the Half-Moon in Little St. Mary's Lane. Porter invited several people to meet Čapek at the Half-Moon, including P. M. S. Blackett, C. P. Snow, I. A. Richards, Michael Ramsey (later Archbishop of Canterbury), and Kingsley Martin (later an author and editor of the *New Statesman*, 1931-60).

p. 80   *kiss the hand of the Vice-Chancellor*: Čapek was in Cambridge for Commencement Tuesday when university degrees were conferred on 'commencing' bachelors.

p. 80   *the Cambridge rabbit*: Čapek and Vočadlo met Dr. Antonín Hanák at Cambridge where he was doing research into the function of haemoglobin in the spleen.

p. 82   *the Wallenstein hall*: Wallenstein (or 'Waldstein') Palace was built in Prague between 1623 and 1629 for Albrecht of Wallenstein, an ambitious general and a key figure in Czech history. The palace's largest space is the main hall which has a vaulted, stuccoed ceiling with a painting of the apotheosis of Wallenstein as the god, Mars.

OUR PILGRIM VISITS SOME CATHEDRALS

p. 84   *la'ma sabach-tha'ni*: 'Eli, Eli, la'ma sabach-tha'ni?': 'My God, my God, why hast thou forsaken me?' Christ's words on the Cross, Matthew 27.46 and Mark 15.34.

p. 85   *something left by the Romans*: this could be any of
         several sights including Newport Arch, the East Gate,
         the Lower West Gate, part of the original city wall and
         ditch, or Fossdyke Navigation, the oldest canal in
         Britain.

p. 86   *St. Cuthbert*: both St. Cuthbert's and the Venerable
         Bede's remains were removed to Durham several
         centuries after their deaths. Cuthbert was a famous
         miracle worker and Bede the author of *Historia
         Ecclesiastica Gentis Anglorum* (731).

JOURNEY TO SCOTLAND

EDINBURGH

p. 88   *Mr. Bone*: James Bone (1872-1962) was London
         editor of the *Manchester Guardian* from 1912 to 1945
         and author of the book, *Edinburgh Revisited*, 1911
         (republished as *The Perambulator in Edinburgh*,
         1926). Bone sent Čapek a copy of his book in June,
         1924. A translation of Čapek's sketches was first
         serialised in Great Britain in the *Manchester
         Guardian*, though the translator, Paul Selver, made
         no acknowledgement of this in his translation and
         indeed omitted this direct reference to 'Mr. Bone'.

LOCH TAY

p. 92   *Karel Toman*: properly Antonín Bernášek (1877-
         1946), the author of, among other works,
         Melancholická pout' (1906), *Sluneční hodiny* (1913)
         and *Měsíce* (1918).

p. 92   *Otokar Fischer* (1883-1938): a literary historian, Professor of German Literature at Charles University, literary and theatre critic, translator, poet and playwright. From 1935 Fischer was artistic director at the National Theatre in Prague where he presented Čapek's last plays. He also translated works by Goethe, Heine and Villon.

p. 93   *There is a hole there*: according to local legend, the pit was reserved for the execution of members of the gentry while commoners were hanged from a simple oak tree.

p. 93   *Campbell*: Finlarig Castle was the seat of the Campbells of Glenurquhay (or 'Glenorchy') and was built by the seventh Laird of Breadalbane, Sir Duncan Campbell (c. 1553-1631), by 1609. Duncan was a cruel, bloodthirsty chief, popularly known as 'Black Duncan of the Cowl' and 'Black Duncan of the Castles'. However, there are no statues at Finlarig Castle, the tale of the sharp-tongued woman is not known there and Marquis Ballochbuich may not have existed at all.

'BINNORIE, O BINNORIE'

A refrain from an old Scottish ballad, 'The Two Sisters'. There are several versions of the 'Binnorie' form of the ballad with differing refrains and differing spellings of 'Binnorie'. Čapek's version seems to be one transcribed by Bruce and Stokoe in 1882.

p. 100 *inverness*: an inverness is a sleeveless cloak with removable cape.

TERRA HYPERBOREA

'Land Beyond the North Wind': in Greek legend the Hyperboreans were a blessed people who lived beyond the north wind ('Boreas'). Mortals could not visit them and they lived in perpetual spring and sunshine.

p. 102 *Skye*: actually, 'Skye' may come from the word 'sgiath', meaning 'wing', after the shape of the island.

p. 102 *Aan Reidhe Mhoire*: this is Čapek's spelling, though the correct transcription may be 'An Réidhe Mhóir' or 'An Réidhe Mhoire'.

p. 103 *King Haakon*: Haakon IV (1204-63). Haakon died in the Orkney Islands after fighting to protect Norwegian territories of which the area around Kyleakin was one. The castle was Dun Akin, meaning 'Haakon's fort'.

p. 104 *a lady with a Greek profile*: this is Čapek's own translation, from a letter of October 6th, 1924. The lady was Mrs. Seton-Watson, wife of R. W. Seton-Watson (see note to p. 138).

p. 104 *Tha tigh'nn fodham, fodham, fodh'm...*: the refrain from 'Ailean Muideartach', a song by John MacDonald. The song is a celebration of Allan MacDonald of Clan-Ranald who was killed at the battle of Sheriffmuir in 1715.

'BUT I AM ANNIE OF LOCHROYAN'

This is closest to a line from an old Scottish ballad, 'The Lass of Lochroyan'. In the ninth verse Annie proclaims, 'But I am the Lass of Lochroyan'.

176

p. 106 *Mělník*: a small town directly north of Prague and situated on the confluence of the Elbe and the Vltava.

p. 107 *Vltava*: this is the Czech Republic's and former Czechoslovakia's longest river. It is also a common symbol of national identity, most memorably in Bedřich Smetana's symphonic poems, *Má vlast* (My Homeland).

p. 107 *Wenceslas Square*: see note to p. 63.

p. 107 *Vyšehrad*: a historical part of Prague which is particularly dear to Czechs as the site of much Czech legend and consequently a place of great importance to nineteenth century Czech nationalists. Vyšehrad Cemetery contains the remains of many famous Czechs, including those of Čapek himself.

p. 107 *Petřín hill*: a large assemblage of hills overlooking Prague and situated beside Prague Castle, the seat of the Czech presidents. It appears several times in Jan Neruda's marvellous *Tales of the Little Quarter* (1878). Čapek had a flat in the Little Quarter, where he was once a close friend and neighbour of Edwin and Willa Muir, the British translators of several works by Franz Kafka.

THE LAKE DISTRICT

p. 111 *Thirlmere and Grasmere and Windermere*: Čapek added the word 'lake' to each of these place-names, perhaps for the benefit of his Czech readers, although 'mere' means 'lake'.

177

NORTH WALES

p. 116 *Luke XII.54*: Čapek incorrectly gives the reference, 'Luke XIII.54'. Luke XII.54 reads: 'He also said to the multitudes, "When you see a cloud rising in the west, you say at once, 'A shower is coming'; and so it happens."' (RSV).

p. 116 *Lliwedd*: one of the principal heights of Snowdon. It is pronounced 'Looeth'.

p. 116 *Moel Offrwm*: this is near Dolgellau and means 'Mount of Sacrifice'.

p. 116 *Cwm-y-Llan*: a green hollow.

p. 116 *Llyn Ffynnon-y-gwas*: a lake.

p. 116 *Crib-y-ddysgl*: another of the principal heights of Snowdon.

p. 117 *Llanfairprllgwyngyllgogerychwyrndrobwllllanty-siliogogogoch*: This apparently means 'St. Mary's Church in the hollow of white hazel near a rapid whirlpool and the Church of St. Tysilio near the red cave'. It is usually indicated on maps and signposts as 'Llanfair P.G.'

LETTERS ABOUT IRELAND

p. 121 *the island in question*: Great Blasket Island, off the south-west coast. The Blaskets have been un-inhabited since 1953.

p. 122 *the Dukeries*: the territory of Sherwood Forest, named after the five dukes who owned most of the area.

BACK IN ENGLAND

PORTS

p. 128 *Captain Marryat*: Frederick Marryat (1792-1848), a distinguished naval officer and adventure novelist. Čapek enjoyed Marryat's writing so much that when he suggested creating a Czech library of English and American authors he wanted an illustrated copy of a work by Marryat to form the first volume in the series.

p. 128 *on account of some congress or royal visit or whatever it was*: a visit by King George V to mark the completion of a part of Liverpool's Anglican Cathedral. The Cathedral was completed in 1978.

p. 128 *the baths of Caracalla*: these were built in 217 A.D. by the Emperor Marcus Aurelius Antoninus Caracalla, one of the cruellest, most corrupt and most dissolute of the last Roman emperors. In their day, the baths were the most sumptuous in Rome. They were destroyed by the Goths in the sixth century A.D.

MERRY OLD ENGLAND

p. 133 *Wyatt*: James Wyatt (1746-1813) was an architect and renovator who restored Durham, Hereford, Lichfield and Salisbury Cathedrals, as well as Windsor Castle, Westminster Abbey and Magdalen College, Oxford. He was known by some as 'the Destroyer'.

p. 134 *Princetown prison*: Dartmoor Prison, originally built to hold prisoners from the Napoleonic wars.

OUR PILGRIM NOTICES THE PEOPLE

p. 135 *Dr. Bouček*: Václav Bouček (1869-1940) was a Czech lawyer and politician who was an expert in English and American law.

p. 137 *St. Julian*: St. Julian Hospitator, subject of Flaubert's tale, *La Légende de Saint Julien l'Hospitalier* (1877), and of the stained-glass window in Rouen Cathedral which partly inspired this tale.

A FEW FACES

p. 138 *Mr. Seton-Watson*: Robert William Seton-Watson (1879-1951), Masaryk Professor of Central European History at the University of London, 1922-1945, and Professor of Czechoslovak Studies at Oxford University, 1945-1949. 'Scotus Viator' was an early pseudonym.

p. 138 *the archangel Gabriel*: the archangel Gabriel is most obviously an intermediary and interpreter. This is the role in which Seton-Watson particularly served the Czechoslovaks and Central Europeans generally. During the First World War he was in direct contact with Czechoslovak political figures in exile and represented the Czechoslovak case for independence to the British government. Between 1916 and 1920 he was founder and co-editor of *New Europe* and was a member of the Intelligence Bureau of the War Cabinet and of the Enemy Propaganda Department.

p. 138 *a house on the Isle of Skye*: 'House Akin'.

p. 138 *a history of the Serbs*: probably *Sarajevo (a Study in the Origins of the Great War)*, published in 1926.

p. 138 *waterproof boys*: one of these, George, became professor of Russian at the University of London.

p. 138 *Mr. Nigel Playfair* (1874-1934): in the spring of 1923 Playfair produced Čapek's *The Insect Play* at the Regent Theatre and *R.U.R.* at the St. Martin's Theatre.

p. 140 *a slightly official situation*: a lunch given by P.E.N. on 3rd June, 1924 at which Čapek and the Rumanian Queen were Guests of Honour.

p. 140 *Viktor Dyk* (1877-1931): a Czech poet, playwright, novelist and nationalist. He was imprisoned by the Austrians in 1917 for his anti-Austrian journalism. After the foundation of the Czechoslovak Republic in 1918 he became a member of parliament and later a senator. He was also, like Čapek, one of the first members of Prague P.E.N.

p. 141 *I didn't see him again*: Čapek was very disappointed not to see Chesterton again nor to be invited to his home at Beaconsfield. He was invited to G. B. Shaw's home at 10, Adelphi Terrace and H. G. Wells's home at Easton Glebe.

p. 142 *a quiet spinet*: at the end of Čapek's and Vočadlo's visit to Shaw's home, Shaw played some music by Mozart on the spinet as a tribute and a farewell. Mozart had found a very appreciative public in Prague in 1786 and wrote *Don Giovanni* for Prague's Nostic (later 'Estates') Theatre. This was first performed on 29th October, 1787.

p. 142   *Rodin*: Rodin had sculpted bronze and marble busts of Shaw in Paris in 1906.

ON BOARD THE SHIP

p. 148   *Holland*: see note to p. 25.

p. 149   *Ik zal nog eens terugkomen*: I will come back once more.

YOU ENGLISH

p. 151   *The Athenaeum*: see note to 'Clubs'.

A SPEECH FOR BRITISH RADIO

This was written at the insistence of Mary Campin, whom Čapek had met in Cambridge in 1924, and was broadcast at 7.30pm on 19th February, 1934 as 'The National Character—Views from Abroad'. The reader was Mr. R. A. Rendall. It was printed in full in *The Listener* on 28th February, 1934.

p. 156   *'How do you do,' he said affably, 'Have you been to China?'*: Sir Martin Conway, a travel writer whom Čapek met at a dinner given by Violet Hunt on 20th June, 1924.

p. 156   *the Great National Reservation of the Anglo-Saxons and Caledonians*: presumably Čapek's own humorous title for Great Britain.

p. 156   *Girgenti*: otherwise known as 'Agrigento', on the southern coast of Sicily.

p. 158   *in their present tense there are both present and past ages*: a reference to the English Present Perfect

Simple ('I have done') and Present Perfect Continuous ('I have been doing') Tenses. Both of these denote a past activity or experience which has some important relation to the present.

p. 160 *Eddington*: Arthur Stanley Eddington (1882-1944) was Professor of Astronomy at Cambridge University. He proposed the notion that outer galaxies are receding from one another.

p. 164 *Perdita*: a character in *The Winter's Tale* who was brought up in Bohemia, one of the two provinces of the modern Czech Republic (the other being Moravia) and home to its capital, Prague. 'Perdita' means 'lost one'. In Shakespeare's time the idea of Bohemia having a coast was a common joke and Shakespeare may well have used it to remind spectators that the play was above all a fantastical entertainment, as indeed do the play's title and several explicit comments by Shakespeare's characters. Čapek also referred to Shakespeare's 'mistake' in his address to P.E.N. on 3rd June, 1924 which *The Times* printed almost in full.